COOL ANTHROPOLOGY

Cool Anthropology

How to Engage the Public with Academic Research

Edited by

KRISTINA BAINES AND VICTORIA COSTA

UNIVERSITY OF TORONTO PRESS
Toronto Buffalo London

ISBN 978-1-4875-0653-7 (cloth)   ISBN 978-1-4875-3437-0 (EPUB)
ISBN 978-1-4875-2441-8 (paper)   ISBN 978-1-4875-3436-3 (PDF)

Library and Archives Canada Cataloguing in Publication
Title: Cool anthropology : how to engage the public with academic research / edited by
   Kristina Baines and Victoria Costa.
Names: Baines, Kristina, 1973– editor. | Costa, Victoria, editor.
Description: Includes bibliographical references and index.
Identifiers: Canadiana (print) 20220141266 | Canadiana (ebook) 20220141363 |
   ISBN 9781487524418 (paper) | ISBN 9781487506537 (cloth) |
   ISBN 9781487534370 (EPUB) | ISBN 9781487534363 (PDF)
Subjects: LCSH: Public anthropology. | LCSH: Communication in anthropology. | LCSH:
   Mass media and anthropology. | LCSH: Anthropology – Research. | LCSH: Anthropology –
   Methodology.
Classification: LCC GN398.5 .C66 2022 | DDC 301.01 – dc23

We welcome comments and suggestions regarding any aspect of our publications – please feel free to contact us at news@utorontopress.com or visit us at utorontopress.com.
Every effort has been made to contact copyright holders; in the event of an error or omission, please notify the publisher.

We wish to acknowledge the land on which the University of Toronto Press operates. This land is the traditional territory of the Wendat, the Anishnaabeg, the Haudenosaunee, the Métis, and the Mississaugas of the Credit First Nation.

University of Toronto Press acknowledges the financial support of the Government of Canada and the Ontario Arts Council, an agency of the Government of Ontario, for its publishing activities.

Funded by the   Financé par le
Government   gouvernement
of Canada   du Canada

ONTARIO ARTS COUNCIL
CONSEIL DES ARTS DE L'ONTARIO
an Ontario government agency
un organisme du gouvernement de l'Ontario

For all those who have pushed for change and a more just society whose names and works we may not ever know

Contents

Preface

When we first started Cool Anthropology, we never intended to write a book, especially one published by a university press *for academics*. We were really interested in creating things *other* than academic books – installations, art, experiences, interactive websites, community workshops, photo essays. We had lots of ideas. Victoria loves ideation. With a background in technology, art, and activism, she brings her diverse professional network, intellectual creativity, community organizing skills and practical know-how, like web development and media production, to the partnership. Kristina brings anthropology – theoretical frameworks and grounded ethnography. Her comprehensive training – a four-field model BA and MA, an MSc in medical anthropology, and doctorate in applied anthropology – provides a deep understanding of anthropological concepts and missteps, as well as the methodological foundation to co-create projects with communities. We felt an ethical obligation to leverage our access and resources to lift community voices and the weighty stories they were telling us, as well as an urgency for academic research to be more easily accessible beyond academic spaces. Others were feeling it, too. We knew we could not do this alone and, through our projects, we connected with those already doing the work and those wanting to do the work, many of whom are contributors to this volume, and our partnership became a collective.

When we began to discuss putting together this volume to share some of the cool work anthropologists and their collaborators were doing, we heard a lot about how this was such a timely project. Truth is, many anthropologists, some quietly and others with more fanfare, have been thinking about, writing about, and *doing* the work of engaging outside of the academy in wide and varied ways for many years. While we have worked to provide an expansive perspective about public engagement in terms of the modalities and approaches highlighted, it is critical to recognize that the call to engage multiple publics with academic research is a long-standing, ongoing endeavor.

Cool Anthropology – and cool anthropology – encompasses aspects of what might be termed public anthropology, engaged anthropology, or even applied or community-driven anthropology. While we are in the mindset, in the spirit of anthropology's roots in holism, of not needing to label or place these projects under one descriptor, we acknowledge that we all owe intellectual and practical debt to those who have carved these different spaces represented by these labels. Some of our authors are essentially public intellectuals and bring their work into public conversations while others design their projects to explicitly address community needs and perspectives. We embrace Haugerud's 2016 definition – "public anthropology … encompass[es] knowledge production by professional anthropologists that is intended to reach beyond disciplinary specialists, and usually beyond the academy" – but push against the exclusivity of "knowledge production" by professionals, asking ourselves how engaging communities as both producers and consumers of academic research helps us not just share anthropology better, but also *do* anthropology better.

The *cool* in Cool Anthropology, the name of this volume and our collective, grew out of a public fascination for all things anthropological – the actual fascinating and very important research many anthropologists do and their uncanny ability to obfuscate and bury it in jargon. Anthropology is fundamentally grounded and community driven. As a discipline, it aims to be responsive to the needs of communities and accountable to its own ethical standards – standards that change as anthropologists learn from the past and integrate methodologies that engage with these new understandings. The range of methods deployed by anthropologists, alongside the foundational holism of the discipline, provides a deep understanding of human life. *Cool* in this context is not frivolous, but rather built on a foundation of rigor. In this sense, all anthropology is cool, not just the anthropology that explicitly calls itself public, engaged, applied, or community driven.

We are not aiming to make the case for public anthropology with this volume. This case has been made in rich and discursive ways by scholars with diverse and deep understandings of anthropology's historical successes and failures in the different aspects of community work and public engagement (see Borofsky 2019; Eriksen 2006; Kirsch 2018; Lamphere 2004; Low 2007; Mullings 2015; Pandian 2019; and others).[1] We come from a moral and philosophical place of believing that academic research, and anthropological research in particular, can and should be produced and disseminated in ways that engage multiple publics beyond those in traditional academic spaces. We explicitly recognize that academic spaces and disciplines have a long and documented history of perpetuating colonial hierarchies, privileging particular perspectives, methods, and means of dissemination that exclude much of the public. Anthropology has a long history of propping up exclusive knowledge systems through the "Othering" of communities as objects of study and interpretation. Reckoning with our disciplinary history is an ongoing process – one that we believe the project of public, engaged, applied, and community-driven anthropology continues to take part in and explicitly reflect on. We hope that anyone coming to this volume has thought deeply about what a decolonizing effort in anthropology might look like and hopes to learn ways to further this effort here. We believe all authors in the volume engage with the problematics of anthropology's history, some more explicitly and all through how they write about their processes of public engagement. It is our hope that you use their stories to address the potential spaces in your own work where you may be privileging voices and/or perpetuating silences.

How do we know that this effort is worthwhile? How do we measure the efficacy of an engaged, public scholarship? There is an element of assessment and evaluation built into all of the chapters; however, the

---

1 Robert Borofsky, *An Anthropology of Anthropology: Is It Time to Shift Paradigms?* (Kailua: Center for a Public Anthropology, 2019); T.H. Eriksen, *Engaging Anthropology: The Case for a Public Presence* (Oxford: Berg, 2006); S. Kirsch, "Experiments in Engaged Anthropology," *Collaborative Anthropologies* 3, no. 1 (2010): 69–80; S.M. Low, "Claiming Space for an Engaged Anthropology: Spatial Inequality and Social Exclusion," *American Anthropologist* 113, no. 3 (2011): 389–407; Louise Lamphere, "The Convergence of Applied, Practicing, and Public Anthropology in the 21st Century," *Human Organization* 63, no. 4 (2004): 431–43; L. Mullings, "Anthropology Matters," *American Anthropologist* 117, no. 1 (2015): 4–16; Anand Pandian, *A Possible Anthropology: Methods for Uneasy Times* (Durham: Duke University Press, 2019).

discussions go beyond what might be thought of as traditional success metrics – for example, numbers of clicks or attendees. Defining success in entering the popular consciousness – creating shifts to make space for anthropological ways of thinking – is not easy. Our authors have been candid about how they overcame, circumnavigated, or were halted by challenges. To be frank, we don't think failure or obstacles are discussed enough in the academy. Success is an ongoing process, and the seeds sown by these authors will grow over the years – with you, as well as those you will influence and inspire with your work. While we realize particular data might influence funders and other opportunities, we tend to move toward decolonizing our own success metrics, believing in the importance of pursuing these less tangible, immeasurable, generational effects of our work.

We asked each contributor to this volume to tell their story, understanding that there were very few linear paths to this work. We wanted to provide a series of guidelines, blueprints, and structured ideation – a "how-to" guide to accomplishing this work. To that end, we asked the contributing authors to answer a specific set of questions in their chapters:

- Who is your "public"?
- How did you get started?
- Which specific relationships inside and outside of anthropology fuel this work?
- Which technologies/modalities do you use?
- How did you find support: funding, respect, clout, for career, world at large?
- How did you find and engage your audience?
- What challenges did you encounter?
- Was your vision realized?
- What lessons did you learn to inform further projects?

Some authors answered these very explicitly while others addressed these questions through their narratives, giving us a window into their process. Our goal is for you to take cues from our experiences – and inspiration – and find your own strategic partners and path. While supports like the American Anthropological Association's document for communicating public scholarship to tenure and promotion committees have been available for some time, much of the public engagement undertaken by anthropologists is still not widely acknowledged by the academy – or funded. We are still on the front lines of this culture shift, and we are all in this together. With your research, and some of the concepts in this volume, we hope that you will build your own blueprint and pay it forward by making it accessible to those scholars coming up behind you also looking for a way to take part in public, accessible, and engaged scholarship.

While we have edited these chapters for clarity and cohesiveness, we purposely kept this to a minimum so as not to flatten or remove individual voices. There is not one way to do this work and we wanted readers to have the opportunity to share in the very personal, emotional journeys recounted by our authors. We have sought to represent both recognized leaders in public anthropology, like those with online platforms, and those using different modalities, including print journalism, virtual reality, interactive installations, visual art, design, sound, feature film, and more.

We consider how anthropologists can engage with non-anthropologists – how we can break the closed circuits of the discipline – and some of our authors have found ways to accomplish this on their campuses and in their classrooms. Consider that teaching outside of the anthropology department is getting anthropology into public spaces. We all have different capacities and access to resources (time being, perhaps, the most important), so we wanted to provide a variety of examples, hoping some will meet you wherever you currently are, with whatever capacity you bring to the mission. In putting together this volume, we sought to include a diversity of both modalities and ways of engaging with those modalites. The contributions are not meant to be exhaustive in any way but instead representative of the kinds of ways that might work for you, the kinds of public spaces you might think about, the kinds of partnerships you might make, and what challenges you might encounter along the way. We have organized the volume into four parts: Imperatives, The World Wide Web, Reimaging Public Spaces, and Creatives.

In Part One: Imperatives, the authors discuss their approaches to addressing the real need for anthropology to engage with the current moment/s in real time. Anthropological projects, even public-facing projects, typically operate on an extended timeline. In this section, the authors discuss how they have used real-time modalities – journalism, social media, public lectures, and interactive installations – to insert anthropological research into their responses to conversations around social issues. The urgency in this work builds on understandings that an insertion of research into these conversations is both ideological and practical.

In Part Two: The World Wide Web, the authors discuss how they have used the online space to reach a wide audience with anthropological writing. They discuss how they conceptualized and created their own blogs, websites, and online magazines as spaces for accessible, jargon-less writing to reach a wider readership both within and outside of anthropology. Writing for online spaces addresses two broad issues in academic writing: the paywalls of academic journals and the academic writing style these journals have historically published. The authors in this section share how they have both found spaces for their own writing and supported students and other academic colleagues in transforming their own writing for these and other public spaces.

In Part Three: Reimaging Public Spaces, the authors discuss how they reimagined their classroom spaces to engage students in non-disposable assignments in public spaces and reach wider audiences. The undergraduate classroom is perhaps the most accessible and powerful public space. Very few undergraduate students will go on to become anthropologists; however, they can bring the tools and understandings from anthropology into whatever careers and public spaces they enter. The authors in this section engage specific publics with collaborative student projects, demonstrating different ways of engaging with them and their communities using photography, installations, virtual reality filmmaking, and participatory design. Through these student/community collaborations, the authors reimagine how anthropology can enter and transform public spaces within and outside of the university.

In Part Four: Creatives, the authors discuss how they have used art, and collaborated with artists, to inform creative projects with anthropological research. Art, in a broad sense, seeks to stimulate discussion, often through an explicit visceral or emotional response. While this response may seem qualitatively different from that sought from the dissemination of academic research, these authors argue – through their discussions of visual art and installations, soundscapes, feature film, and comics – that art engages the public in the same concepts and understandings as academic research in ways that are more accessible and immediate. The embodied experience of engaging with concepts through creative modalities has the power to change conversations in different ways than academic reading and writing.

The contributors to this volume are radicals breaking down the walls of the academy – often, as you will read, with little support of any kind. We see this volume as building community – the community that so many of our contributors note they so desperately needed. But anthropologists cannot reach a wide public alone. Building partnerships with people who have different perspectives and skills is critical and will serve the goal of making your research more understandable, relevant, and meaningful, and collaborating with people outside of anthropology and the academy becomes a tangible step to getting your work *out there*. Cool Anthropology would not exist without a creative technologist thinking anthropological research and concepts were valuable for the world, and she had to find her way to anthropology in order for that to happen. Seek these connections. To view updated and interactive examples of the authors' works, follow the QR code to the digital companion. And reach out! You are part of the community now.

Kristina Baines
Director of Anthropology, Cool Anthropology
Associate Professor of Anthropology, CUNY Guttman

Victoria Costa
Director of Cool, Cool Anthropology

Acknowledgments

We are grateful for the collaborations and connections that have made this volume – and Cool Anthropology in general – possible. First and foremost, we would like to thank the community members who participated in the research that is the fundamental component to all of the projects shared in this collection. Without you sharing your stories so generously with anthropologists, there would be no stories to tell. A special thank you from us to Basilio Teul, Eluterio Mes, Florentina Pop, Florencio Canti, Martha Pop, and Ezekiel Canti.

Thank you to the anthropologists, artists, friends, and colleagues who championed our work from the beginning and were fundamental to us growing and continuing – and for still being here with us. You believed in us as much as you believed in the mission and contributed to the work without any compensation, and we really could not have done it without you. Special thanks to Rebecca Zarger, Daniel Lende, Heide Castañeda, Antoinette Jackson, Kerry Hawk Lessard, Anne Pfister, Alison Cantor, Mabel Sabogal, Nolan Kline, José Hasemann, Carylanna Taylor, Etel Kerchhoff, Alicia Ebbitt McGill, Marisa Macari, Amy McLennan, Paige West, Hannah Graff, Michael Harris, Carrie Ida Edinger, Doug Reeser, Celeste Bacchi, Lisa "comagirl" Parrot Perz, Deanna Charles, Gina Margillo, Monique Boileau, Vaimoana Litia Makakaufaki Niumeitolu, Daniel Velasquez, Nick Palughi, Cassie "Kazilla" Williams, Gregg Deal, and Elizabeth Briody.

We have had too many inspiring conversations and informal mentorship moments to name, but we are incredibly grateful to you all, including Alisse Waterston, Leith Mullings, Greg Downey, Darlene Dubuisson, Aaron Hockman, Mark Schuller, Janelle Baker, Krista Harper, Laurie Medina, Alayne Unterweger, Liz Bird, Baird Campbell, Bianca Williams, Niel Tashima and the National Association for the Practice of Anthropology (NAPA), Chip Colwell and the *SAPIENS* team, Emily Martin, Maria Vesperi and the *Anthropology Now* team, Tom Miller, Kristin Koptuich, Agustin Fuentes, and all the authors in this volume.

Many thanks to the Wenner-Gren Foundation for supporting our work in so many ways, and our particular gratitude to Michael Muse, Judy Kreid, Mary Elizabeth Moss, Leslie Aiello, and Danilyn Rutherford.

To the CUNY Guttman students who used their ethnographic skills and worked with us to shape the projects we write about in this volume, we thank you for inspiring us to think more deeply about how we define and interface with our publics: Shenice Greene, Maria Isabel Parada, Sade Miles, Onasis Cirineo, Dwayne McCallum, Lakiera Taylor, Deja Clarke, and Hannia Delgado.

Thank you to our editors at University of Toronto Press: Carli Hansen, who inherited the project but has enthusiastically and diligently led us to the finish line, and Anne Brackenbury, who initially understood and championed the project and supported us as we shaped it into what it was to become. And our sincere appreciation goes out to four anonymous reviewers, who helped us to clarify what we were really hoping to achieve with this volume.

Bringing this volume together during a global pandemic was also made possible in part because of our amazing neighbors in Sunnyside, Queens. We are so fortunate to be a part of this community. Special shout out to Sunnyside Community Services, the 45th Street Composters, 49th Street, the Sunnyside Community Garden, and Uncle Jimmy!

Finally, we would like to thank our family for their support. Costa's parents, Amy Linden and Peter Costa, instilled an intellectual curiosity and civic responsibility in Costa that inspires her to forefront ethics and a collective spirit in all of her pursuits. Baines's parents, Thalia Baines and Keith and Thayer Baines, fostered a global perspective and a "can-do" attitude in her. A special thank you to Thea Irene Zigoris for her generosity and belief in us and our projects.

And the final special thanks goes out to Cooper Myers, who was a child when we started all of this and grew up alongside Cool Anthropology. Your moms appreciate your love and support (and your recent Anthropology minor!) and are hopeful we have shown you how dedication to one's goals and values can grow and be met over time if you keep at the small steps.

PART ONE

Imperatives

Making Anthropology Cool: Translating Anthropological Research and Concepts Using Multimedia

Kristina Baines and Victoria Costa

We will never forget that moment in 2012 when we found ourselves carefully balancing several five-gallon buckets on a red velvet and shiny golden luggage cart, pieces of freshly ground corn suspended in liquid sloshing over the sides, through the grand lobby of that San Francisco hotel. We had just completed our first live event, what the American Anthropological Association called an "innovent" at the time, during which participants learned about Baines's Embodied Ecological Heritage (EEH) framework (see Baines 2016, 2018), which she developed while conducting research in a Maya community in southern Belize and had just written about in her dissertation, "Good Men Grow Corn" (see Figure 1.1). We presented EEH through the lens of community members, artists, and anthropologists who had all contributed their work to answering the question "What is embodied ecological heritage?" through their varying personal modalities, including anthropological research, painting, filmmaking, and multimedia installation. As Costa was deeply intertwined in the Miami art scene at the time, the vision was to blur the lines between academic research dissemination, experiential, multisensory education, and a cool art space. Instead of sitting and listening to a talk, participants were invited to listen to a looped video of anthropologists and community members discussing

Interaction how EEH plays out in their lives and work while they were grinding fresh corn, sorting corn seeds, and sipping not on wine, but on the corn drink, or *sa*, they had created before engaging with the art in a more traditional gallery setting. The framework's emphasis on embodiment set the tone for the entire project and has influenced each of our subsequent works.

If attendees embodied an experience, we posited, they would be much more likely to remember it than if they just listened to a talk. And if they remembered it, they would be much more likely to talk about it in another space. And that is what we wanted to do: change conversations.

Cool Anthropology was not born that day, but that awkward walk across the hotel lobby was a turning point for us. We were committed to challenging hierarchies and promoting equity through storytelling and were just beginning to understand how much potential community-generated/community-centered projects have to make grounded, anthropological research accessible and relevant outside of the traditional academic environment. We wanted to explore nontraditional means of dissemination, and this was the beginning of a real awakening, both practical and intellectual, of what would become one of the primary methods of our work: the live installation.

> *If attendees embodied an experience, we posited, they would be much more likely to remember it than if they just listened to a talk. And if they remembered it, they would be much more likely to talk about it in another space.*

Our theoretical orientation trended toward the phenomenological, with a focus on the lived experience of both the research participant and the researcher. Live events went a good distance toward creating that experience, purposefully blurring the lines between data collection and dissemination. From a more practical perspective, we checked our ambition that day. While we were solidifying our commitment to experience and community, walking through the hotel lobby and packing those same buckets and artwork into friends' cars to set up the same event at a San Francisco community garden (Figure 1.1), and getting everything back on a plane to go home (where we installed it at subsequent events (Figure 1.1)), it helped us consider how to streamline – and eventually fund – our process. Wrapped up in our learning curve was how the stories told and created at the events could live on in other spaces and eventually live on without us.

THINGS TAKE TIME

Eight years prior, in 2004, at Costa's first American Anthropological Association (AAA) meeting, we had eagerly attended a session entitled "Making Anthropology Cool." We were both already dedicated to getting great ideas out into public spaces. Costa is a creative technologist who enjoys leveraging her tech skills and experience in instructional design to produce transmedia stories for audiences across physical and virtual spaces. At the time, she was new to anthropology but excited about the insights it could offer to her perspective, generally speaking, and her creative pursuits, more specifically. Baines – having attended many gatherings where each time someone asked what she studied or what she did, and she said, "I'm an anthropologist," the response would almost always be, "Oh! Cool!" – was eager to collaborate with the goal of *actually* making her research cool, meaning useful beyond a handful of other academics who might show up at one of her talks. And, thus, our critical partnership began. Together, we work with community members to encapsulate important ideas, and then we work together to figure out how to tether the project to the broad interests of the public and current events. Costa, who would become our "Director of Cool," is the visionary – she figures out how we tell our stories. Her background in agile development, instructional design, and artistic communities helps her conceptualize our projects and adapt them for different audiences. She also manages our organizational strategy, the teams of academics, artists, and community members, has her hand in the audiovisuals and written materials, and much more. Baines, as the "Director of Anthropology," keeps everything grounded with anthropological research and concepts and provides us with the institutional credibility we need to gain access to academic and scientific networks, funding, and opportunities.

Cool Anthropology was not really born that day, either, but the conversations about the value of public-facing scholarship and the value of the anthropological mindset in producing real understanding in the world became more and more frequent. Humility, empathy, immersive

coolanthropology.com presents

Re/consider Dissemination - Crossing Traditions

Embodying Ecology Through Experiential Art

Participate: Wednesday. 12 December 2012. 5:00-7:00pm.
@ The Gray Mocking Bird Community Garden in Lake Worth, FL

with a special planting of Mopan Maya corn seed at 6:30pm

Check coolanthropology.com/reconsider-dissemination for more
information and details about Pop-Up events around town.

Figure 1.1. Our first installation, "Crossing Traditions," at the American Anthropological Association's annual meeting in 2012 (*top*); the Hayes Valley Community Garden in San Francisco in 2012 (*opposite page, top*); and the South Florida Slow Food Conference (*opposite page, bottom*) in 2012.

methods, holism – we recognized the ethical obligation to share these tools, and the results of inquiry using them, with more than just a few people sitting in a conference session or the few dozen people who find an academic paper. Anthropologists, even great anthropologists, needed help figuring out ways to do right by their own cool research.

Late in 2010, conversations and ideas finally coalesced in the form of our website, coolanthropology.com, which Costa built to design and house the interactive teaching tool Baines developed as part of her last graduate seminar before her dissertation fieldwork. The seminar, on research ethics, inspired Baines to dream up a "choose your own adventure" style activity based on real-life fieldwork scenarios. Costa chose to create the website and tool with Wordpress because it is a mission-driven, open-source web platform, which meant that we had immediate access to a wide range of plugins developed by other Wordpress users around the world that exponentially expanded the capacity of our website and projects without any increase to our budget or time. Using the blog category hierarchy feature embedded into Wordpress and an image slider plugin, participants read through brief situations and then could choose the decision they would make based on their understanding of anthropological ethics and their obligations to their research participants. Each decision was analyzed using the AAA's code of ethics as the user is guided through the pros and cons of each choice. Ethics, we figured out, allowed us to present what we would later think of as "big anthropological concepts," like cultural relativism and the strength of deep and detailed ethnographic methods, in engaging ways. The ethics tool was provocative but, ultimately, it was designed to be used by students. While students are often our first "public," we knew we wanted to grow in ways that would bring discussions around these "big anthropological concepts" to different kinds of "publics" even if we hadn't clearly defined who those were. Ten years later, we have a better idea, but this is an ongoing and evolving question for us – for better or for worse.

COOL, CREDIBLE CONCEPTS

While Cool Anthropology has evolved in so many ways over the last ten years, our mission has remained remarkably steady. As we slowly built out coolanthropology.com, we also started social media pages, first on Facebook and Twitter and eventually on Instagram. We carefully selected images and text for each space. Baines's fieldwork photo of the hand of a Maya girl holding five freshly harvested black beans seemed to work: personal yet ubiquitous, visually appealing yet not sensational. For our tagline, we wanted to reinforce the idea that making anthropology accessible and useful to a wide audience didn't mean watering it down or sharing surface-level anecdotes. Costa came up with our "cool, credible concepts" tagline to clearly capture the level of rigor behind the research we shared. This was, and continues to be, a critical point. We set out from the very start to address the issue head on: Using jargon and unintelligible sentence structure does not make our research better, more credible, or more meaningful. It is possible – and now we are bold enough to say, imperative – that research be understood beyond a small group of specialists. Not only is it imperative, it is a fundamental responsibility of researchers, particularly as academia contends with its ongoing colonial legacy.

Over the years, we have invited anthropologists – beginning with those in our immediate circle – to experiment with us in multiple forms of dissemination. For the first installation, they recorded videos explaining what the terms "embodiment," "ecological," and "heritage" meant to them. We asked community members from the Maya village in southern Belize where Baines had lived while conducting her doctoral fieldwork to do the same. We asked artists Costa knew from her work in the Miami art and music scene to interpret the terms through creative modalities. Our friends from all locations were supportive and thought that our ideas were cool. We did not really need to convince or cajole. In fact, we have almost exclusively received positive support and feedback for both our individual projects and the wider mission. From this first event, even from the first website teaching tool, other anthropologists have willingly participated, congratulated us on executing much-needed public-facing projects, and excitedly shared our work with others. Anthropology *is* cool, they agreed, and they were willing to help us prove it.

Of course, it was not exactly that simple. Despite all of our commitment to rigorous scholarship and support from the academic community, there were, and still are, many times when this public-facing work felt like something that was an "add on" or an "extra" for Baines and our collaborators. Even to us, who were deeply committed to the mission, it felt challenging to carve out the time to really give it the attention it deserved. We would take installations to conferences and meet scholars who were excited to interface with our work. We evangelized anthropology and discussed how general public inquiries and curiosities should be responded to by anthropologists. But when we would invite people to write for our "Ask the (Cool) Anthropologist" column on our website, we often ended up on their back burners. Momentum built very slowly.

As Baines started her tenure-track position in 2014, the reasons why the contributions did not always match the enthusiasm became clearer. Even at her innovative institution, which prides itself on an experiential and applied learning ethos, it was unclear where Cool Anthropology's public-facing projects fit in the academic world. From live and virtual multimedia installations to explanations and answers to anthropological questions answered on the website, our academic system had no "bucket" in which to clearly place this work. It is research dissemination, but it is not a peer-reviewed article. It is teaching, but it is not in a classroom for credits. It is service to the community, but it is not reviewing or editing for a journal. We knew from the response to our work that the culture of what should count as academic work was changing, but the system was not keeping up. Honoring the importance of anthropological research through making it cool for the public often meant doing double work: creating more traditional outputs for your institution and then, if there is time, working on public-facing projects. We have considered a more formalized peer review process or an online, open-source journal as possible ways forward, and we remain hopeful that our work, and this volume, keeps pushing the academic needle.

TIME IS NOT MONEY

While it is true that scholars bend to the conventions of academic work because they would like to keep their jobs and pay their bills, there is more to the financial story of public work. On the timeline of our Cool Anthropology trajectory, we have almost always worked for free. Baines now has an academic salary, but expenditures routinely outweigh its parameters. Any funding for salaries we pass to our students and collaborators, often thinking how we could reach a wider audience, engage with more people or dive deeper if we had the time and space to not worry about funding the next steps.

Our second installation, the "Road of Development," probably our most ambitious yet, debuted at the AAA meetings in Chicago in 2013, while Baines, a newly minted PhD, was on the job market. It was entirely self-funded and involved an incredible amount of logistical and intellectual preparation. Academics and artists contributed their thoughts

How can change happen?

on how seven stages of development impact communities across seven stations lined up in the grand hotel ballroom. Each of these stations included an easel with a frame housing a tablet with prerecorded video from an academic – portrayed as art worthy of framing – talking about how they observed the impacts of development through their ethnographic research. A curtain backdrop displayed infographics Costa had created with an artist, Monique Boileau, along with two other artistic contributions: a series of collages by Nick Paliughi and what would become the key icon of our project: the "super heroes" of development "trading card," a collaboration with pop artist ComaGirl. In the spirit of having participants embody an experience rather than just listen, look, or read, each station had an activity that participants were asked to do: stack and measure ramen noodles to guess how many you could buy for the same cost as a bunch of bananas, fill a seed bomb, smell a spiritual perfume, and more. We bought all the items, paid the extra luggage fee, edited video in a friend's apartment (no money for a hotel room), set up and broke down everything ourselves. After break down that day, we crawled into a coat closet near the ballroom and fell asleep. We call this our humble beginnings. The installation was very well received and we began to hear a buzz about more people, different people, who wanted to get involved in our projects. Regardless, the time, cost, and energy needed to tour with this work prohibited us from taking it to as many places as we would have liked or that would have made equity of the incredible labor so many people contributed. We needed more than just great energy, scholars, and artists willing to participate. We needed collaborators – different collaborators. Collaborators with money.

Our turning point (one of them) came in 2015 when the Wenner-Gren Foundation commemorated their seventy-fifth anniversary with the launch of _SAPIENS_, their online magazine dedicated to public scholarship (read more about it in chapter 6) and their Innovations in the Public Awareness of Anthropology grant opportunity. We applied and were awarded the grant to fund our next project, "Shifting Stereotypes." Inspired by the burgeoning social movements #BlackLivesMatter, #ChangeTheName, and #NotOneMore, we created an embodied experience during which participants were asked to read quotes aloud that exemplified stereotyping language spoken by actual people in positions of power. Baines now had students who

Figure 1.2. "Super heroes" of development trading cards designed for the "Road of Development" installation by ComaGirl and Victoria Costa, 2013 (*top*); the "Road of Development" installation, Chicago, 2013 (*bottom*); the "Road of Development" flyer (*opposite page, top*).

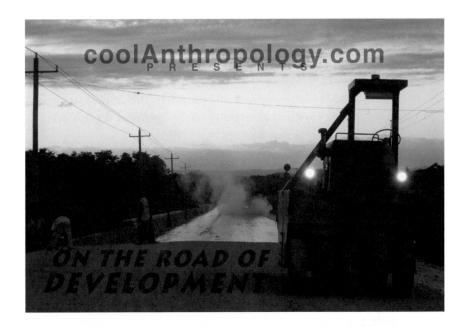

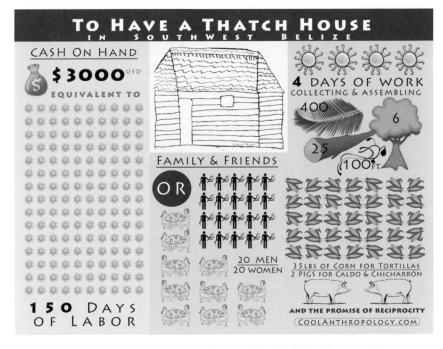

Figure 1.3. Infographic designed for the "Road of Development" installation by Victoria Costa and Kristina Baines, 2013.

could travel with us to facilitate the installation, and the funding allowed us to have a wider reach. We recorded video of both the quote reading and the exit interviews, which Costa conducted with each participant. We asked everybody: How did you feel when you said these words out loud? Has anybody said anything like this to you before? Have you ever said anything like this to anybody? What do you think about stereotyping?

A second iteration debuted the following year and asked participants to pile sort terms that came out of the exit interviews and explain their sorts to student interviewers. We explored the methodology through its original application as a tool of cognitive anthropology, which we set against the first iteration's focus on embodiment. The funding, and our more developed understanding of how to sustainably tour with an installation, allowed this project to reach more and more publics. Some of our conceptual thinking – like framing tablets to convey the artistry of anthropological thinking, which worked beautifully in the "Road of Development" but needed careful handling – had to be pared down. Our "Shifting Stereotypes" posters could be rolled up and carried in a small tube or downloaded by anyone anywhere. We really wanted to open source as much of this project as we could. We facilitated both installations in a variety of locations and were extended invitations to speak about its development. Every location and audience brought a completely different tone to this work – the AAA meetings had a totally different vibe than the public community college or liberal arts university. The independent website for the project evolved over time and through careful consideration. As feminist and queer movements have emerged since the inception of the project, we have felt compelled to expand upon it – we are hopeful people will leverage the open-source nature of the work to help frame other important discussions around stereotyping and social movements.

As 2015 became 2020, the project transformed into an interactive documentary, bringing anthropological and community perspectives on stereotyping to an even wider public. We developed a curriculum, annotated bibliography, and downloadable package, including all of our installation materials (posters, interview questions, pile sort activity, etc.). In the spirit of open education and open-source development, this is something we now do for all of our projects. We also were awarded a small innovation grant to host a hackathon and develop our own open-source digital pile-sorting tool as a Wordpress plugin. This was a great opportunity to evangelize anthropology and socially conscious ideation and projects to computer science departments and their students across several CUNY colleges. Social science and computer science students teamed up together to storyboard their concepts and design wireframes. Costa and another web developer, Chris Chalmers, took their work and produced a working plugin. Now, any researcher anywhere can use the tool and conduct digital pile sorts, and any visitor to the "Shifting Stereotypes" website can digitally participate in the experiential activity and contribute to the story/our data set. We workshopped how to teach the activities at the Society for Applied Anthropology meetings and have since made everything available for free online. Our goal is to have this project reach high schools, colleges, and community centers all over the United States so that learners can explore anthropological concepts – such as structural violence, microaggressions, and historical trauma – and draw connections to the quotes, the positionality of people in power, and their own lived experience.

The grant from Wenner-Gren also came with its strong network of support. Long after that funding was spent, the folks at the foundation championed our mission through attending events, distributing flyers, retweeting our content, publicizing our workshops and events, and more. Collaborators and champions are essential in this work. While it is more challenging to shift our perspective that this is critical work that should not be tied to a paycheck, working with students and young scholars has really motivated us to find ways to avoid asking them to give their insights and energy for free. Small grants from Baines's institution have helped us give stipends. Baines won a fellowship that included funding for students, and we used that to support our social media manager and a graduate fellow for public scholarship to transform and expand the "Ethnography Matters" project (described below) for Instagram, Twitter, and Facebook. For that project, we were a core team of four, two anthropologists, Baines and graduate fellow, Baird Campbell, as well as two non-anthropologists, Costa and social media manager, Hannia Delgado. It has been amazing to work with these young minds and to be able to pay them for their contributions. Campbell just graduated from Rice University with his PhD in anthropology. His research involves social media

Figure 1.4. Flyer for "Shifting Stereotypes," 2015.

movements and digital ethnography, his perspective and experience relating to engaged and public scholarship inspire us, and his background as a high school-level classroom teacher helped us flesh out a solid open-educational curriculum and introduction to anthropology for our website. Delgado has a bachelor of business administration with a concentration in marketing management and digital marketing and helped us navigate strategies to increase engagement (read: the efficacy of our efforts). Engagement – audience members interacting in some way with our content (e.g., commenting and sharing) – is more important to our mission than passive clicks or likes, and this is at the forefront of any conversation related to our goals and values. Creating content that is intended to exist in different spaces, online and off, has presented a lot of opportunities to be creative with transmedia storytelling and consider generational impacts. It is also an exciting challenge to carefully consider how the same work could potentially be used across different spaces, audience perspectives, and moments in history.

Although she's an honorary anthropologist now (no, really, it happened in a basement at Oxford University), Costa has, from the beginning, brought a perspective that was impossible for Baines to see alone. In addition, she also brought creative and logistic networks, as well as practical and technical skills that Baines did not have.

As a scholar and a researcher, you should focus on what you do well and let your collaborators focus on what they do well. You don't need to learn how to code, how to become a video editor, or penetrate the Miami art scene, and non-anthropologists bring a fresh perspective to research, design thinking, and analysis.

⌊Working with others outside anthropology is <u>critical</u> to expanding your reach⌋ As a scholar and a researcher, you should focus on what you do well and let your collaborators focus on what they do well. You don't need to learn how to code, how to become a video editor, or penetrate the Miami art scene, and non-anthropologists bring a fresh perspective to research, design thinking, and analysis.

Collaboration is key.

SPECIFIC ETHNOGRAPHIES, BROAD ISSUES

Bringing the benefits of anthropological research to the public – and doing this across spaces – is an interest that has grown into an imperative for us. Engaging deeply with the "Ethnography Matters" project has us more resolute in our thinking and articulation of our mission. "Ethnography Matters" was developed as a way to address our frustration and bewilderment at the media frenzy unfolding in 2016. We asked ourselves what ethnographic methods might contribute to conversations about fake news in the context of the jarringly dichotomous media coverage of the new president. We had a sense that contributions ethnographers could make would be both broad and specific.⌊Broadly, the "ethnographic lens" helps us assess information in a way that is explicitly non-dichotomous.⌋ It reveals nuance that seems so lacking in public media discourse. The ethnographic process is also very specific, and it was these specific details of what ethnographers do that we aimed to capture in the initial live installation in December 2017. We designed and printed posters on which we invited participants moving through the installation to answer questions about their ethnographic processes:

How can we make ethnography more palatable/adapted for non-anthropologist?

- What is the most important quality of an ethnographer?
- Which ethnographic methods are you using?
- Where have you done ethnography?
- Where do we need ethnographers right now?
- How does ethnography matter?
- What would it take for society to respect and utilize ethnographic methodologies?
- In which ways can ethnographers and their research inform the popular narrative beyond the academy?
- What else do you have to say about ethnography?

Two undergraduate student researchers also asked participants if they would like to answer the questions on camera and captured informal video responses on tablets. Participants were enthusiastic. We found that they were doing really important research – research that could reveal deep understandings and truths that people seemed so desperate to find. We continued collecting the answers to these questions on the webpage and have since encouraged anthropology departments to download and print the posters to have these critical, detailed conversations in their institutions. We hoped these conversations would be ongoing across multiple spaces. Our #EthnographyMatters social media campaign featured direct, attributed quotes about the ethnographic process or research relevant to current events and online trends. Our strategy with this transmedia project was to introduce ethnography and its importance to the public – using the anthropologists' words and ideas we had collected in person and online – while lifting the voices of intersectional ethnographers.

What we learned from this installation, and from the subsequent cross-media engagement with it, is that the public benefit in learning anthropological research is not simply that it is cool and research should be shared and widely available (it should be). While we draw from studies from across anthropology and the social sciences, the deep insights gleaned from ethnographic research can and do offer a rigorous alternative to, or at least a contextualization of, much of the information that circulates in the popular media. Ethnographic insights can help us all better understand the world and our place in it. Ethnographic data are simultaneously detailed and specific, and they also provide a broad blueprint to consider the world through a

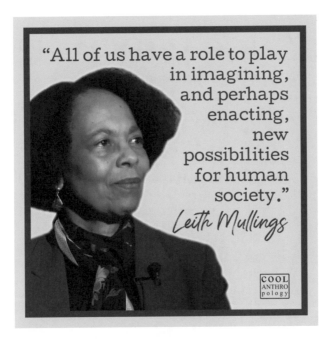

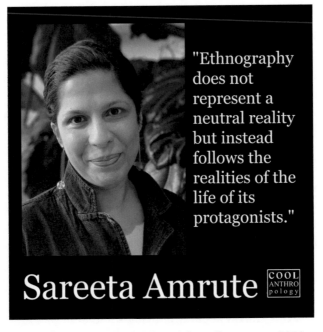

Figure 1.5. "Ethnography Matters," social media memes, 2020.

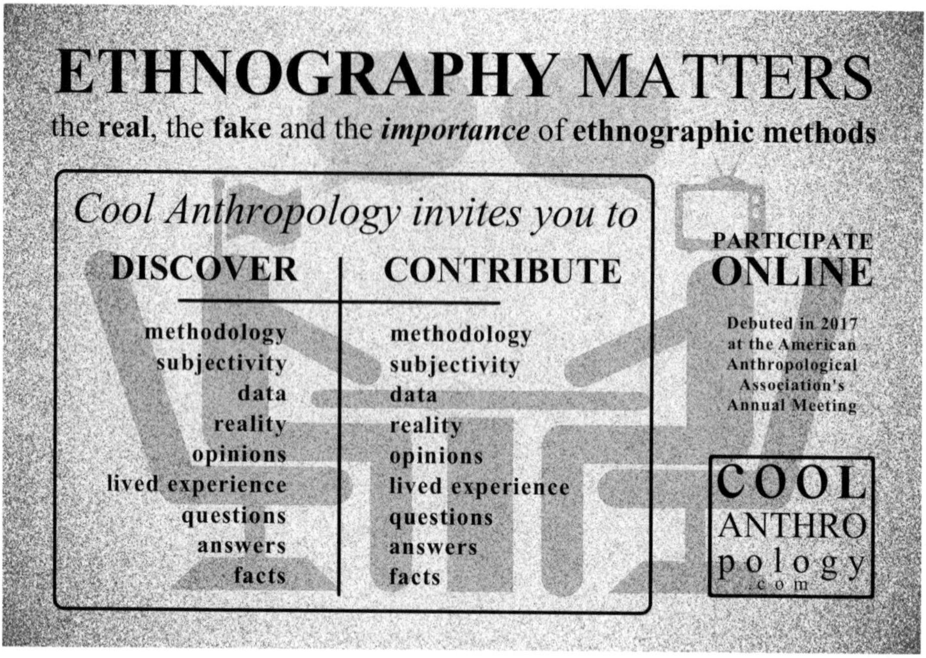

Figure 1.6. Flyer for "Ethnography Matters."

different lens or from a different perspective. They have the power to provide the nuance that makes the difference in understanding. They are community-based, rich in detail and, because of this, we argue they are more trustable.

When grounded ethnography forms the basis of participatory design, community members do not just make contributions to the research or learn from the dissemination of that research, they are project co-creators. In 2015, we received a grant to enable community members in a small Belizean Maya village to organize and fund a short film documenting the Deer Dance. Community members worked with the producers (us) on the story they wanted to tell through the film, and students from the village worked alongside the filmmakers to record the four-day event. The role of the film was not simply to document the dance as it happened, but to relay how community members felt about the practice and documenting of the dance. Community members were adamant about producing something they could show their children in the years (most every year) they could not afford the cost of the costumes, transportation, and feeding the village, which Positive Legacy funded that year. Anthropology has long wrestled with the problem of putting so much power in the hands of the ethnographer as it relates to how the community is represented. Participatory design and innovative research dissemination methods go some distance to addressing this power imbalance.

While we have always considered making anthropological research available to a wide audience as a critical part of what might be described as social justice work, espousing the benefits of ethnography in revealing deep truths has become more explicit in recent years as media corporations have been consolidated,

Social media provides an alternative, one that we use with increasing care and frequency, helping us meet people where they already are. In this way, it can be a democratizing space. It can also be a dismissive space, allowing for important research to be passed by.

obscuring more and more voices. Social media provides an alternative, one that we use with increasing care and frequency, helping us meet people where they already are. In this way, it can be a democratizing space. It can also be a dismissive space, allowing for important research to be passed by while competing with cute cat pictures, potentially cheapening its value or flattening its epistemological depth.

We thought about this tension long before we began the ramping up of our social media presence. It is one that all public or engaged scholars should grapple with and address. The threat of research being dismissed – by both the public and the academy – for being in contested and fraught public spaces is a real concern.

While the nuts and bolts of actually getting research out into public spaces while maintaining methodological and analytical rigor are translatable across many disciplines, developing this process with Baines's research as a starting place set the tone for a spirited evangelism of anthropology. Anthropologists are well-equipped to speak to the many social issues facing communities today. If we consider much of the conflict in the world is due to differences in cultural ideas and practices, it makes sense that researchers trained in cultural analysis, and following the basic tenet of cultural relativism, would be highly qualified to contribute to addressing pressing public issues. We have long wondered why policymakers and journalists have not more often turned to anthropologists to speak to these issues. We hear from economists, political scientists, even sociologists, but rarely anthropologists. We have often asked ourselves, "why?" and have come to the conclusion that anthropologists often do not incorporate public applicability into their training. This is changing but "traditional" programs often encourage students to enter academic conversations in lieu of entering public ones. It is our hope that these conversations can somehow be merged rather than ranked. We would like to see a fluidity of dissemination made the norm.

As we were confined to virtual spaces in 2020, our focus on public issues such as racism, health, climate change, media, and politics has become more explicit, with our message targeting a wider audience. While we have always addressed "big" issues in our work, the installation format allows for both an embodied experience and a personal conversation, with us and/or our student facilitators. This allows us to add nuance in a way that virtual spaces may not allow. The intimacy of in-person ethnography is mirrored in the blurred data collection/ dissemination space of the installation, where the activities and conversations deepen the experience and often change the installations in real time. Although the publics are different in a virtual space, there is an overlap. In our virtual events, we tend to focus on how intimate ethnographic studies can shed light on broad issues, and we focus on big anthropological ideas. As we have hosted and been invited to lead discussions on how we engage in public scholarship, our public has grown even further. This book is an example of that.

FLEXIBLE YET RESOLUTE

Building Cool Anthropology, and creating cool anthropology, has been the ultimate teacher. We learned flexibility in the most tangible of ways. In a very practical sense, we never know, even at the AAA meetings, what our live space is going to be, and, consequently, the details of how we will set up and how participants will embody the experience. As we conceptualize our projects, we have even less knowledge about other venues and the publics they will attract. We marry Costa's background with agile development with Baines's training in the rigorous flexibility of fieldwork. While all our work is developed collaboratively by us (an anthropologist and a non-anthropologist), the live installations shift in focus depending on both the space and the audience. After we pushed the bucket of corn drink across that hotel lobby in San Francisco, we set up the same installation at a community garden built on an abandoned highway off-ramp downtown. There, it was not as easy to separate the activities from the "art gallery" as we had done in the hotel room. Instead of being projected on a sheer screen between these two sections, the video of community members and anthropologists talking about what embodied ecological heritage meant for them was looping on one of our computers tucked into the safety of the tool shed. Art hung from trees and was balanced against garden perimeters. The mess of the corn drink was less of a concern.

Though live and virtual (and virtual live) installations take a lot of planning, particularly if you are generating unique art and graphics (which we always are) and traveling with your equipment (which we always are), you cannot plan for everything you will encounter in the spaces where your work lives. With an academic paper, there is a little more control, a little more knowledge of how and by whom your work will be read and received. With public work, even when we are standing next to it, facilitating, discussing, explaining, and recording exit interviews, there are always surprises. Our goal for Cool Anthropology is that it lives on without us. Like a child that you birth and/or nurture, you can only build a solid foundation and see what happens when the world adds its influence. And, like parenting, even with the myriad challenges and disappointments, it continues to be worth it. We are often surprised by who connects with our work and in which ways. If there is one thing we have learned from anthropology, there is not just one "right way."

FOR DISCUSSION

1 Our projects are co-created with different types of collaborators – community members, artists, students – and we are committed to open education/science/source code/etc. In which ways does co-creation challenge the notion of "expertise" and how might we address concerns that our research is no longer "ours"?

2 Part of our focus as public scholars is to use our research, access, and resources to address important social issues of the moment. In which ways is public scholarship anti-racist and decolonial in nature, and how can we use participatory design and/or other methods to address hierarchies?

3 Installations take a tremendous amount of research, planning, labor, and coordination, but they typically are not subject to the same kind of peer review that academic evaluation is based on. How might you make the case for a public installation as a form of scholarship to a thesis/dissertation committee or a tenure/promotion committee?

4 We often talk about meeting people where they are – physically (or digitally), in terms of their thinking and experience, etc. – and they are certainly on social media platforms. In which ways is social media both a democratizing and dismissive space?

5 Most of our projects are designed to exist in multiple spaces, for varied audiences. As we parse out specific elements and publish them on- and offline, some of our content has been accused of "epistemological flattening" by other scholars. How can a poster, meme, or 260-character statement maintain academic rigor?

What makes an expert?

REFERENCES

Baines, K. 2016. *Embodying Ecological Heritage in a Maya Community: Health, Happiness, and Identity*. Lanham: Lexington Books.
Baines, K. 2018. "But Are They Actually Healthier? Challenging the Health /Wellness Divide through the Ethnography of Embodied Ecological Heritage." *Medicine Anthropology Theory* 5, no. 5. https://doi.org/10.17157 /mat.5.5.461.

CHAPTER TWO

Getting Knowledge from the Ivory Tower to the Street: Making Anthropology Matter

Agustín Fuentes

Racism, inequality, rampant nationalism, sexism, and a multitude of other damaging processes are challenged, engaged with, and disarticulated by anthropological knowledge. Anthropology is not only cool, it matters. But not if it stays in the ivory tower. The copious data and important insights from the broad study of humans past and present, and that of our closest relatives, provide a critical toolkit to tackle many of the contemporary crises facing humanity. However, the challenges in translating and disseminating such toolkits to the broader public are substantial and the impetus to take them on is nowhere near as common as it should be. In this chapter, I offer some personal experiences and political analyses of the translation process and a suite of methodological suggestions that can help make anthropological knowledge more accessible, more effective, and more exciting to those outside (and inside) of the academy.

WHY?

White supremacists chug milk on YouTube in the misguided belief that their lactase persistence (the ability to produce the enzyme lactase into adulthood) is a hallmark of a particular European ancestry, homogeneity, and superiority (it is not) (Harmon 2018).

[handwritten margin note: Interesting topic. Look to find more info]

The International Association of Athletics Federations (IAAF) has decided that women with "too much" testosterone can't compete as women (Pielke et al. 2019), assuming that the androgen hormone is the defining factor for sex, athletic ability, and "femaleness" (it is not) (Karkazis and Jordan-Young 2018).

The manifesto by a white, male Google engineer tells us that compared to men, women are more open to feelings than ideas, more open to people than things, show gregariousness rather than assertiveness, have higher rates of neuroticism, and are more prone to anxiety. Moreover, it says that men have a higher drive for status and are more capable of dealing with stress and technological challenges, and these general personality trends, the author states, are biological and cultural universals (they are neither). Inherent in the manifesto is the assumption that human males and females experienced different patterns of evolutionary pressures and thus evolved different systems of response and perception (they did not). And that is why the author believes Google's attempt to develop a more level structural landscape of access will fail (Fuentes 2017).

[handwritten margin note: exact? how can these become common sense?]

Does this all sound familiar? All are arguments embedded in erroneous notions of human nature, human evolution, and human biology. Given the political and social state of the United States and the world, and the widespread ignorance of biological and evolutionary processes, none of this is at all surprising. There is no way around the density of misinformation about human biology and evolution in the world today. Combining the emergence and ubiquity of the internet with the pervasive momentum of nationalism, misogyny, racism, and intolerance generates a slew of "information" that permeates almost every corner of people's lives. One need not look to these extreme cases because even seemingly banal books about humanity, images in advertising, and a plethora of other media outputs act to perpetuate and promulgate inaccurate representations of human diversity, human history, and contemporary patterns and processes of the world.

[handwritten margin note: How do these become common sense to us?]

In today's reality, an accurate and factual understanding of the data involved with human diversity (cultural and biological) is critical. These facts are indeed all around us and fairly easy to access, but they remain in competition with much noise, obfuscation, and intentional lying, meant to steer conversations, ideas, beliefs, and actions in specific directions. I do want to be clear, science is always political; I am not asserting some special bias-free zone for anthropology, or scientists in general. How we, as scholars, talk about data, how we contextualize it, and what we do and do not present has implications. There is no neutrality for humans – we are all biased and all have agendas.

However, the agenda of anthropology provides a particularly important lens, and access to a range of critical types of information, that can act to ameliorate and push against harmful and hateful information, assumptions, and assertions – particularly as it consciously and reflexively grapples with its colonial legacy. However, on average in the twenty-first century (at least so far), anthropological voices are heavily underrepresented in the public sphere. Rather, the dominant voices on anthropological topics are those

I do want to be clear, science is always political; I am not asserting some special bias-free zone for anthropology, or scientists in general. How we, as scholars, talk about data, how we contextualize it, and what we do and do not present has implications.

with the popular appeal of simplistic and often anti-anthropological "translators" of science; for example, books like historian Yuval Noah Harari's *Sapiens: A Brief History of Humankind,* psychologist Steven Pinker's *The Better Angels of Our Nature: Why Violence Has Declined,* and political scientist Charles Murray's *Human Diversity: The Biology of Gender, Race, and Class.* Many such books top the anthropology rankings on Amazon, despite being openly antagonistic to anthropology, having large swaths of anthropologists disagreeing with them, and multiple published anthropological refutations or suggested corrections to their contents.

The world of the twenty-first century, what many call the Anthropocene, is overflowing with meaning and crisis, and it gravely needs anthropological voices and practices. Anthropological input on biomedicine and racialized neo-eugenics are needed to overcome substantive obstacles to social justice, health, and well-being. The global reach of crises erupting over nationalism, (im)migration, (bio)politics, and inequalities are the norm in the twenty-first century, and we need to engage with them. Biodiversity and biotransport, agro-manipulations, and multispecies ecologies infuse the daily experiences of humans globally, and anthropology contains a multitude of toolkits and perspectives that would enable more effective, and sustainable, interfaces with these issues.

Talked about in our top 100

How does Anth. from the Past damage Anth. now?

Mainstream media, disingenuous politicians, legal scholars, psychologists, political scientists, and economists continue to dominate the public discourse on life, law, economics, sports, entertainment – the panoply of human experience. We are in the midst of a substantial (re) writing of histories, presents, and futures. The twenty-first century needs anthropological investigation, translation, influence, and action. Let anthropology respond. Loudly. Publicly. Interestingly. Entertainingly.

We are in the midst of a substantial (re)writing of histories, presents, and futures. The twenty-first century needs anthropological investigation, translation, influence, and action. Let anthropology respond. Loudly. Publicly. Interestingly. Entertainingly.

CONTEXT

There are three particular arenas where I focus the majority of my translating anthropological knowledge from the academy/profession into public spaces and mindsets: blogs/SciComm essays, public lectures, and Twitter. The bulk of my translations focus on breaking down, and refuting, many of the myths about human nature, and thus human evolution, that are prevalent and popular in regard to the topics of race, sex/gender, and what it means to be human. Basically, my goal is to show that the available data we have about human biology, human history, human evolution, and human cultural diversity refute and/or complexify these myths. My take is best summarized by the opening to my 2012 book, *Race, Monogamy, and Other Lies They Told You*:

> Three major myths – about race, aggression, and sex – have a negative impact on our society and inhibit an accurate understanding of what it means to be human. These myths create a false set of societally accepted "truths" that in turn cause a range of problems for us. The myth that humans are divided into biological races – that Black, White, Asian, etc. are natural categories – helps generate and maintain intolerance and inequality, and leads to difficulties in creating and sustaining communities in our increasingly diverse society. The myth that removing the constraints of culture and civilization reveals the innate, violent beast within us (especially in men) restricts how we can relate to one another, encourages

fear, and enables an acceptance of certain kinds of abuse and violence as natural or inevitable. The myth that men and women are
dramatically different in behavior, desires, and perspectives due
to natural differences in "internal wiring" facilitates poor intersex-
ual relations, creates and maintains sexual inequality, and causes a
range of problems for individual men and women laboring under
a preconception about who and how they are supposed to be.

The core specific themes that I most often translate for the academy
to the public are (1) race is not a valid description of human biological
variation but it is real as a social, historical, and structural process – as
such, racism is systemic and can have biological effects; (2) there is no
biological coherence to "male" and "female" brains or any simplicity
in biological patterns related to gender and sex, but gender/sex matters deeply for humanity; and (3) simplistic stories about human evolu-
tion/nature are almost always wrong and the reality of the human story
is complex, messy, and marvelous.

HOW

In my attempts to "get knowledge from the ivory tower to the street,"
I draw on published research from anthropology, biology, psychology,
history, and beyond, state-of-the-art professional society statements (e.g.,
the American Association of Physical Anthropologists [AAPA] 2019 and
the American Society of Human Genetics [ASHG] 2020), the public
writings of many of my colleagues, my own background and educational
experiences, my teaching, and my own research. This means that I must
read across multiple areas/disciplines within the sciences and humanities, continue to modify my own understandings and positions as more
information and assessments emerge, and be constantly open to the reality that there are always data and analyses with which I am not yet familiar and for which I need to watch
(Fuentes 2018a, 2019).

*One must be as current and fluent
as possible in the contemporary
landscape of primary research
and theoretical debates. And one
must be ready to be, or have been,
wrong.*

I wholeheartedly believe that
to be a scholar who engages in the
work of translation to the public,
one must be as current and fluent as

possible in the contemporary landscape of primary research and theoretical debates. And one must be ready to be, or have been, wrong.

Let me offer some brief notes as to how this pans out in the loci of
translation in which I participate.

BLOGS/SCICOMM

In 2012, I was invited to write for *Psychology Today* and for about five years
(2012–2017) I maintained a blog on the site (which is still up: https://
www.psychologytoday.com/us/blog/busting-myths-about-human-
nature). Since 2012, I have blogged/written for *PLOS SciComm, Salon,
National Geographic, Scientific American, SAPIENS, Somatosphere, Huffington
Post*, and many other sites. Sometimes I approached these publications
with ideas and sometimes they approached me. I draw from those experiences to offer a few points about my process and what I learned.

Picking a timely topic is often very important as a way to highlight
the relevance of academic knowledge to the broader public (#MeToo
issues, the aforementioned Google manifesto, a white supremacist rally,
racist statements by governmental or other prominent figures, and so
on). Another stimulus for me to write a blog or essay is when a contro-
versial (and in my opinion, wrong or misleading) article or research
finding emerges and gets picked up by a range of media. Common patterns of misrepresentation of key data about humans include the mis-
use of genetic and/or medical studies to support a biological basis for
race (such as the infamous book by former *New York Times* science writer
Nicholas Wade), psychological assertions of certain "evolved" gender
differences that reinforce discrimination and bias (like the Google
memo and all its supporters), researchers offering a "naturalness" or
evolutionary explanation for rape and sexual violence (such as that by
psychologists Randy Thornhill and Craig Palmer (2000)). These topics
resonate with the public, so linking a broader narrative of human evolution, behavior, or variation to something specific in the recent news
cycle is important as it establishes a connection to both the "why" and
the "so what" for readers. In doing so, an anthropologist can offer clarity and correction to false representations of what and why humans are.
But data on human biology, variation, or behavior by themselves, and
even a good anthropological analysis by itself, will do little to engage

or convince most readers to reconsider what they think of as "right," "normal," or "just the way things are." You need to be able to frame and present those data in a publicly engaging and interesting manner.

A good example of this kind of bad science can be found in the assertions made about male and female evolutionary differences in the Google manifesto and the public-facing support of them by evolutionary biologist Jerry Coyne and philosopher Johan Haidt (see, for example, Coyne 2017). Another example is the strident assertions by geneticist David Reich (2018) that he knows better how to discuss and understand human variation and race than do social scientists. The case of misrepresentation of human "progress" by the psychologist Steven Pinker (Weintraub 2018) is another good example. In each of these cases, I, either alone or with colleagues, used blogs as modes of responding and correcting, anthropologically, the misrepresentations of knowledge, data, and reality presented by these scholars and amplified by news media (Fuentes 2017, 2018b; Kahn et al. 2018).

But how does one do this? Blogs tend to be between 800–1,200 words (give or take) and, for me, should have three key parts: hook and punch line, content related to data or understandings of data, and a narrative frame that connects those two and offers a reason (or reasons) why this matters.

The hook and punch line are basically to 1) let the reader know what public information is being tackled, and 2) why that information is wrong and what the right (or a better) answer is. One can immediately see that my blogs are largely reactive to something in the news/public media cycle that I see as incorrect and/or harmful to our understanding of what it means to be human. The exception to that is when I am asked/contracted to write on a specific topic, then the hook and punch line are to lay out what I am writing about and why anyone should care.

One specific aspect I see as very important in the act of translation is the highlighting of other key articles/blogs/essays that do good work in making information accessible. Placing links and/or citations to a small number of relevant, and effective, bits of information acts to both bolster your credibility and assist the readers in engaging in a bit of guided investigation on their own. Some scholarly sources work better than others to bolster and clarify my point of view. So, while the relevant data and analyses might be available in a number of articles or books, I choose to link to, or cite, certain ones that I think will be the most effective if engaged with by the public. This measure of "effectiveness" can simply be well presented and structured arguments, it can be the quality and cadence (narrative flow) of the writing, or it may be the particular frame the author uses to present and discuss the data.

Finally, while I think it can be dangerous to be directly confrontational (calling certain individuals out) as it can turn off some readers, it is important to draw a clear line of contention with those that I disagree with and those that I think are misrepresenting the data on human evolution, behavior, and variation. This is easy if I am responding directly to a statement or blog or essay by someone, but takes a bit more nuance when you want to pull someone in who was not the specific individual behind the key item you are highlighting.

PUBLIC LECTURES

This is the arena in which I have been spending increasing energy and effort. The lectures I give tend to be in two core arenas: university settings and public events/festivals that highlight science, human evolution, and issues of social justice (e.g., race and racism). For more than a decade and a half, I have been invited to universities in the Americas, Europe, and Asia to offer single lectures or series of lectures to students, faculty, and often the public. These are very important opportunities, as the institutional ("ivory tower") sponsorship offers a template of trust that one has sufficient academic credentials to be discussing what one presents. These are excellent venues to engage the public without having to work too hard up front to convince them of your credentials and capacity to convey accurate and important information. My most frequent other type of lecture involves attending and presenting at festivals and public events without university linkage but with themes that resonate with the three areas of focus I outlined previously or in the more general arenas of human evolution or primate behavior and conservation/sustainability. This includes non-university institutions, such as museums, zoos, and aquariums, and even corporate-sponsored public speaker series. These opportunities usually draw on a wider range of the public than the university lectures and thus one has to create a dialogue and presentation content that reaches broadly and at the same time sets you up as an "expert" who has the training, background, and experience to be offering up insights and valuable knowledge.

There is a more recent third type of lecture, the "TED Talk" style, where the presentation is short, more choreographed and follows a certain pattern of delivery and use of imagery. I have done one TEDx Talk and a few related types of presentations, and I would argue that they are largely a hybrid in content and style between blogs and longer lectures and have a range of distinctive characteristics that set them apart. I have not had extensive experience in this area, so I am still working through my methods of delivery and my theory of practice for it. The recent upswing in podcasts is also an area where I am increasingly engaging, but that too is a hybrid of the modes I've just described and I am early into figuring out how to best engage this form of presentation.

The benefit of a lecture versus a blog or essay is the ability to narrate a story live, to offer images, and to craft a more conversational engagement with your audience. For me, this is a great opportunity to perform the act of translation, as I enjoy public speaking and storytelling … and it is storytelling that is critical in public lectures. In a 40–45-minute lecture, I have the capacity to spend more time with the topic, to draw out examples and to illustrate them with powerful images, graphs, and charts (but not too many) while verbally guiding the audience in how they see and interpret the images and concepts I am laying out for them. Much of the core content of my lectures would be the same that I use in the blogs and essays, but the delivery and the time to do it can be quite different.

For me, the most effective translation component of the public lecture is in the Q&A. If you've done a good job of getting across your core points and offer up some data/information in support of them, the audience will have questions of interpretation and clarification. This is when you get to delve deeper into the specifics and elaborate on them in accordance with the questions asked. This enables a broader engagement with the information and enables you to see where your delivery in the lecture worked and did not work, helping you hone the focus/content for the future.

TWITTER

I have now been on Twitter for just over five years and am still in the process of developing methodology and practice. Rather than a social interface in general, I see and use Twitter as a template for translation work and as a mode of connection with a broader research community. Thus, I have a three-fold goal in my use of Twitter:

1 To disseminate information/data to inform both scholars and the broader public of recent and important information via linking to articles, books, essays/blogs, and other websites
2 To initiate or engage in Twitter threads on key topics related to my areas of expertise and interest
3 To follow scholars and other Twitter users I see as sources of valuable information and insight

In undertaking these goals, I do not engage in "flame wars" or other extended Twitter debates. Mainly I've used Twitter as a space to focus on translating data/knowledge on race/racism, human evolution, and the social, ethical, and structural challenges of diversity and inclusion facing the sciences and the academy in general. I see Twitter as a mode of brief and critical information transfers, with the option for momentary back and forth, but I do not think the long, drawn-out and, at times, vitriolic exchanges are of value. When attacked or trolled for a post (which is not uncommon), I generally do not respond or respond once or twice but no more. I have also occasionally reached out to those posting serious disagreements or debates and offered to engage in clarifying discourse off of Twitter.

CHALLENGES

I have had a range of very positive responses to my translation work, but the translation does not always go well. There have been a number of challenges, most learning experiences, some disheartening, and some repulsive.

The one thing that anyone who wishes to do translation of scientific knowledge to the public work around issues of human nature(s), especially race/racism, sex/gender, and human evolution, must recognize is that they will be attacked personally and virulently. Such attacks are often via social media or in emails, sometimes by phone calls.

The mildest are from more structurally traditional academics in the evolutionary and psychological sciences, usually white males (this is,

unfortunately, a salient detail), but sometimes females. These objections
are generally centered on the "reality" of male-female evolved psychological and biological differences and the naturalness of racial divisions
and xenophobia/"tribalism" in humans, all as the result of human
evolution via very specific patterns of natural selection. These are often debates about what evolution is and how we should be modeling it.
Such objections are fine and can help me refine my arguments, except
the few that turn personal, such as when a prominent evolutionary psychologist complained loudly to the Twitterverse that I kept "picking on"
evolutionary psychology unfairly and thus was being unfair and abusive.

[margin handwritten note: Academic evidence?]

The more angry, less useful notes usually come in response to my
public work in the race/racism area, and they range from things like
(these are excerpts from emails I received):

> You are one dumb son of a bitch. You are irrelevant to the human
> race.

> Just so you know, the entire politically motivated "race is not biolog-
> ically real" paradigm is going to come crashing down hard this cen-
> tury. The amount of evidence to the contrary is overwhelming. In 100
> years, people peddling this nonsense will be seen as the next crop of
> Lysenkoists, peddling pseudo-science. Scientists are making fun of
> you behind your back. You people are beginning to be seen as some
> weird fundamentalists.

> You "cultural anthropologists" are probably the most anti-science
> people today in the USA. You have no new ideas so you just want
> to silence the advance of science, usually by repeating worn-out
> slogans such as the Cultural Marxist mantra "race is a social con-
> struct." Most people I know just laugh and make fun of you losers.
> You people are no better than religious fundamentalists, where
> your religion is "race is a social construct." You are the New Crea-
> tionists. Darwin, James Watson, Crick, EO Wilson, WD Hamilton,
> Dawkins and Pinker all accept the biological reality of race. They
> support real science. You people support a fanatical religion.

And so on. There are many much meaner ones that I don't want to
put in print, but you get the picture.

Difficulties in doing so due to other academics perpetuating structures/uising[handwritten margin note]

Most of this I can blow off, some concern me, but the commonalities in the attacks and the fervor of so many, especially around race and sex/gender, remind me that this is not only a serious problem in our society, but that there are many individuals out there right now who hold dangerous and potentially violent views about other humans. This is why public translation work is so important: those voices and views need to be counteracted with facts, analyses, and information that the broader public can use to push back, to understand, and to act for a better society.

Let me also be very clear: the pushback and online abuse that I receive is nothing compared to that received by my female colleagues, especially women of color. Women academics who bravely participate in the translation realm suffer enormously online with direct impact on their personal and professional lives. They receive volumes of hateful, hurtful messages that often contain personally targeted violence. This, again, is a statement about our society and the continued presence of violent misogyny and racism as part of the social fabric. It is also a clear reason why translation work against this matters.

There is another type of challenge that is worth mentioning: institutional and structural conservatism in regard to the topics of race/racism and sex/gender. Erroneous assumptions about human biology and human evolution are baked into US (and much of European) society and it comes to the fore at times even in places one might not expect it. I stopped blogging for *Psychology Today* for this reason and I have had similar contexts/scenarios/interactions with major newspapers and media sites, even in some of the places one might assume are "progressive. Many of those in charge of the structures of dissemination of public translation are, like all of us, products of the society in which they reside. And our society is infused to the core with racist, racialized, sexist, misogynistic structures of violence. Even some of those thinking they are pushing against ignorance are blind to the structural inequities and violences they are part of reproducing. This may be the deepest and most substantial challenge we face in doing valid and effective translation work.

But again, this is just all the more reason for those of us lucky enough to be able to participate in the translation of anthropological knowledge and data to the public should continue doing so.

THE FUTURE

I've laid out what I do and why I do it in regard to translating knowledge from the ivory tower to the public and in the effort trying to make anthropology matter beyond the academy. I am convinced that what anthropology has to offer is both cool and relevant. I am also convinced that the modes I have covered – blogs/essays, public lectures, and Twitter – are valuable and effective modes of doing this translation work. However, this position presents a problem. There are few, if any, PhD programs that train students (or faculty) to engage with these modes of knowledge dissemination and for the vast majority of universities, non-peer-reviewed writing, public engagement, and the use of social media are not explicitly recognized and valued in tenure and promotion criteria. In fact, and unfortunately, there remain many anthropological scholars who think such endeavors should not be recognized as part of the academic landscape. I wholeheartedly disagree. I do not think everyone should be doing this work of translation, but those who wish to, and those lucky enough to be in a position of privilege (like me) to do it, should.

I think it is a moral and ethical necessity that we (in anthropology and the academy writ large) provide usable access to, and engagement with, the knowledge we produce for a broader public. One critical way to do that is to revise our curricula and assessment criteria to reflect the contemporary landscape of engagement by both scholars and the public. We must realize that the challenges of misinformation, discrimination, bias, and violence are too great to ignore. This is not an easy task, as it requires departments and the discipline on the whole to unify around this reality and to structure our internal programs to reflect it, as well as to then convince our institutions that this is a significant aspect of our scholarship and professional activity. Specifically, I think we need to recognize that this type of activity is not "service" but rather part of the actual process of scholarship. Anthropological scholarship does not need to stop at the peer-reviewed article or book with an established university press. A next step is also part of the intellectual process: translation to the public.

This is not a new perspective; in fact, much in contemporary anthropology got its start because of the public nature of our ancestors (Hurston, Mead, Montagu, Benedict, Du Bois), and much of today's anthropology in public is in response to other public scholars we see as

[handwritten margin note: Does it belong in our academic world? Ethics?]

misleading the public. We already do much of this work. I submit that we need to be prepared to do more. We need to train our students (and faculty) to do it (those who wish to), to recognize such activity as scholarship, and to continue to try to use anthropology to effect change.

Zora Neale Hurston tells us that "[a] thing is mighty big when time and distance cannot shrink it." Our obligation as anthropologists to make the knowledge we generate mean something beyond the academy is, and has been, a central factor in our raison d'être. And it's not shrinking anytime soon.

FOR DISCUSSION

1 Racism, inequality, rampant nationalism, sexism, and a multitude of other damaging processes are challenged, engaged with, and disarticulated by anthropological knowledge. Which strategies are effective when deploying this knowledge to those who are engaging in these processes?

2 To engage in the work of translation to the public, one must be as current and fluent as possible in the contemporary landscape of primary research and theoretical debates. One must also be ready to be, or have been, wrong and/or attacked personally and virulently. How should you handle the times when you discover you are or were wrong, or if you are accused of being wrong?

3 Good translations for the public need to have three key parts:
   a. hook and punch line
   b. content related to data or understandings of data
   c. a narrative frame that connects those two and offers a reason (or reasons) why this matters
   How can your research apply this format?

4 Anthropology programs should train students (and faculty) to engage in public knowledge dissemination. Public engagement as anthropological practice should be explicitly recognized and valued in tenure and

promotion criteria. What kinds of training/workshops/
professional development would be useful?

5 The challenges of misinformation, discrimination, bias,
and violence are too great to ignore. Let anthropology
respond. Loudly. Publicly. Interestingly. Entertainingly.
What are some of the reasons people do not engage
in public scholarship, and what would you say to a colleague who tells you they are not interested in public
scholarship?

REFERENCES

American Association of Physical Anthropologists. 2019. "Statement on Race
    & Racism." March 27. https://physanth.org/about/position-statements
    /aapa-statement-race-and-racism-2019/.
ASHG (American Society of Human Genetics). 2020. "American Society of
    Human Genetics Statement regarding Concepts of 'Good Genes' and
    Human Genetics." September 24. https://www.ashg.org/publications-news
    /ashg-news/statement-regarding-good-genes-human-genetics/.
Coyne, J. 2017. "Salon Disses Dismisses Google Memo as 'Biological
    Determinism' That Can 'Slip into Eugenicist Doctrines.'" August 11.
    https://whyevolutionistrue.com/2017/08/11/salon-disses-dismisses-google
    -memo-as-biological-determinism-that-can-slip-into-eugenicist-doctrines/.
Fuentes, A. 2012. *Race, Monogamy and Other Lies They Told You: Busting Myths
    about Human Nature.* Berkeley: University of California Press.
Fuentes, A. 2017. "The 'Google Manifesto': Bad Biology, Ignorance of
    Evolutionary Processes, and Privilege." *PLOS SciComm*, August 14. https://
    scicomm.plos.org/2017/08/14/the-google-manifesto-bad-biology-ignorance
    -of-evolutionary-processes-and-privilege/.
Fuentes, A. 2018a. "Towards Integrative Anthropology Again and Again:
    Disorderly Becomings of a (Biological) Anthropologist." *Interdisciplinary
    Science Reviews* 43, no. 3–4: 333–47. https://doi.org/10.1080/03080188
    .2018.1524236.
Fuentes, A. 2018b. "Enlightenment Now and Empathy Later?" *Somatosphere*,
    September 19. http://somatosphere.net/2018/enlightenment-now-and
    -empathy-later.html/.
Fuentes, A. 2019. "Identities, Experiences, and Beliefs: On Challenging
    Normativities in Biological Anthropology." *American Anthropologist* 121,
    no. 2. https://doi.org/10.1111/aman.13227.

Harmon, A. 2018. "Why White Supremacists Are Chugging Milk (and Why Geneticists Are Alarmed)." *New York Times*, October 17. https://www.nytimes.com/2018/10/17/us/white-supremacists-science-dna.html.

Kahn, J., et al. 2018. "How Not to Talk about Race and Genetics." *Buzzfeed*, March 30. https://www.buzzfeednews.com/article/bfopinion/race-genetics-david-reich.

Karkazis, K., and R. Jordan-Young. 2018. "The Powers of Testosterone: Obscuring Race and Regional Bias in the Regulation of Women Athletes." *Feminist Formations* 30, no. 2. doi:10.1353/ff.2018.0017.

Pielke, R., R. Tucker, and E. Boye. 2019. "Scientific Integrity and the IAAF Testosterone Regulations." *International Sports Law Journal* 19: 18–26. https://doi.org/10.1007/s40318-019-00143-w.

Reich, D. 2018. "How Genetics Is Changing Our Understanding of 'Race.'" *New York Times*, March 23. https://www.nytimes.com/2018/03/23/opinion/sunday/genetics-race.html.

Thornhill, R., and C.T. Palmer. 2000. *A Natural History of Rape: Biological Bases of Sexual Coercion*. Cambridge: MIT Press.

Weintraub, K. 2018. "Steven Pinker Thinks the Future Is Looking Bright." *New York Times*, November 11. https://www.nytimes.com/2018/11/19/science/steven-pinker-future-science.html.

CHAPTER THREE

The Urgency of Now: Crafting and Editing Anthropological Knowledge in Real Time

Maria D. Vesperi

Storytelling and the mediation of cultural knowledge are central to nonfiction genres such as long-form journalism and ethnographic narrative. Bringing the private into the public is central to anthropology, an awesome responsibility but one frequently muted by jargon-defended writing and restricted publication. Barriers to wider audience reception have become increasingly apparent as anthropologists move beyond the academy to seek readerships claimed by other, more polished nonfiction genres. Some problems are obvious: convoluted sentence structure, weak organization, citation jam-ups that impede narrative flow. Others are more subtle and less tractable, particularly those that concern writer isolation, vetting, ethical constraints, and the most slippery of elusive goals, timeliness. In this chapter, I address some of these issues by drawing on my experience as a former journalist, my years as a trustee of the Poynter Institute, and my current work editing print and online submissions for *Anthropology Now*, a journal-magazine and website project that aims to make anthropological knowledge less focused on disciplinary discussion and more accessible to general readers while preserving scholarly integrity.

DEADLINES

"Time has come today." That definitive riff from an old song by the Chambers Brothers still echoes faintly on the airwaves in a psychedelically prophetic, 1960s kind of way. It is also the freshest insight I can give to a nonfiction writer, particularly an anthropologist who hopes to share hard-won knowledge with an eager public audience. Time has come. Today's the day. Tomorrow's too late. Like John Henry and the steam engine, nonfiction writers are locked in a heart-busting race with technology to get the word out first. Journalists, well-conditioned and accustomed to daily deadlines, are usually first out of the gate. Ironically, however, many of the same technological advances that make the newsgathering process faster work against the journalist when it comes to dissemination. Hence the grueling 24-hour cycle with its constant updates.

Time is never, ever on the anthropologist's side when communicating with the general public. Graduate school and work experience offer little support for the urgency that drives a contemporary news cycle. Good fieldwork is slow and immersive; write-up deadlines are self-chosen and weakly enforced. Serious writing is a rusty art, practiced mostly on special occasions; it is not the everyday survival skill upon which professional writers depend. A journalist's gratification is prompt and multifaceted; work is published quickly and acknowledged with feedback from editors, peers, and the public, plus a paycheck.

In contrast, gratification for the anthropologist is deeply, deeply deferred. Publication can be so glacially slow that when an essay or book eventually emerges it can feel like someone else's work – dead-ended by the finality of the written word while the author has continued to, well, live. Feedback is often both minimal and critical and, of course, there is no pay.

The mention of money might stop some would-be storytellers, trained as academics are to believe that the purity of their work will be compromised by selling it. But consider that full-time nonfiction writers don't eat unless their efforts are consistently accurate, interesting, clear, and timely. That's a powerful motivation to do one's best, and better. Anthropologists tend to be solid with the accurate part, but "clear" is problematic and "interesting" can be much too narrowly defined.

This last is because academic readers are a captive, self-selected audience with context-specific tastes such as geographic area and theoretical orientation. So, no matter how painfully obscure and awkwardly stated their content might turn out to be, writers who speak to area specialties and anthropological canon(s) can anticipate at least a core readership. Sometimes reader interest seems as mindlessly knee-jerk as a Beavis and Butt-Head routine: "(snort) He said hegemony!" But no matter, it's published, another line on the resume.

Other nonfiction writers are acutely mindful of their audience, usually before they even propose a subject or accept an assignment. First, they ask: might their readers care about this? If so, to crib a title from French novelist Marie Cardinal, can they find "the words to say it?" Among the most adamant arguments I witnessed as a full-time staffer at the *Tampa Bay Times* concerned whether our half-million Sunday readers would "get" a particular pop culture reference, often a song lyric. Sharp but instructive generational divides were often laid bare by such disagreements. The lesson: just because a reference indexes something to you doesn't make it a clear and effective vehicle for reaching an audience.

Jargon is by nature exclusionary; in academia, it shamelessly flaunts insiders as superior to those who don't get it. But for more general readers, jargon just tags the content as inaccessible.

This feeds into the deadline problem because to be interesting and accurate, a story must be timely. As anthropologists learn early and often, culture is never static. Insights from the field gleaned over time might make one an "expert" in the larger sense, but not necessarily an accurate source of current information. Stuff changes. Accessibility is an issue here, too; the more background needed to bring a topic up to speed, the greater the risk of losing readers in the minutiae.

Writing on deadline takes iron discipline. Journalists have two key resources to enforce it: fear and a supportive team of colleagues. Reporters who routinely blow deadlines get fired – no tenure, no excuse. Hence the fear. Not nice, but it's a supreme motivator. In contrast, as Bruce Grindal and Robin Rhodes once wrote, "An anthropologist is a journalist with a two-year deadline" (Grindal and Rhodes 1987). That makes self-discipline harder to achieve, so best to find like-minded colleagues who can share the urgency of now.

ISOLATION

Trading the newsroom for a faculty office was my biggest challenge in moving from journalism back to campus. The isolation was profoundly de-energizing, and even after 28 years, I rarely close my office door or spend a minute in that serene little room-with-a-view beyond the hours I meet with students. It's too lonely for this team player.

I get more done at home, with people and animals around and a constant multispecies parade past our house near downtown St. Petersburg, Florida. It helps that my husband, Jay Sokolovsky, is an anthropologist, too; our projects are different, but we share the reality-check radar when it comes to whether or not an idea can fly. That's among the things I most enjoy about working with *Anthropology Now* as well – the collaborative spirit that fosters ongoing, productive engagement among writers and editors. Our work is most similar to what journalists call "thumb suckers," well-researched investigative articles or magazine pieces that present complex, sometimes technical content in a way that invites readers in and challenges them to understand. Despite appearances, the label is not derogatory; print and online publications alike have renewed respect for long-form pieces, which are popular with readers – including younger ones. Here's a place where anthropologists who want to reach wider audiences can settle in, ideally with writers and editors who share the same goals.

It helps to join a writing group, preferably one that includes mixed genres where the focus is on craft over content and people are serious about reading each other's work. I belonged to such a group until the untimely death of our organizer, and I still miss the feedback from folks who were working on novels, poetry, and memoir. They were all successful authors, all mercilessly critical of their own writing, and all good at immediately stumbling over the slow spots in mine. It is also useful to take advantage of any and all opportunities to attend writing workshops and seminars and also to brush up on style with guides such as Constance Hale's *Sin and Syntax: How to Craft Wicked Good Prose* (2013). As I tell students in my Newspaper Writing and Production classes, writing is a craft and working to master it is a lifelong project.

GOALS

"A man's reach should exceed his grasp, or what is heaven for?" wrote Robert Browning in 1855, and the same can be asked today of anthropologists who would reach across time, space, and perhaps intention to forge works that resonate with contemporary audiences. Browning's words have been read as a meditation on longing and risk, and here I would like to continue a discussion I began with an essay called "Taking Chances" (Vesperi 2011). I later initiated a column on anthronow. com called "Reach," where I occasionally invited anthropologists to provide their own takes on works singled out for review by anointed art critics and other cultural "experts." I hoped to explore the concept of reach as it describes anthropologists' longing for fresh engagements with ethnographic representation and the risks they take in the process. A stunningly successful example was "Reflections on Kara Walker's 'a Subtlety, or the Marvelous Sugar Baby.'" Anthropologist Elizabeth Chin suggested this one, and Dána-Ain Davis, Gina Ulysse, Antoinette Jackson, Yarimar Bonilla, and Elizabeth herself engaged the topic with powerful, poetically spare commentaries and/or original photos (Bonilla et al. 2014).

Careful fieldwork and insightful theoretical framing cannot stand alone; in a discipline that does not teach its students how to write, one must still tell the story. Telling it well is a desire shared by many, and what follows are a few touchstones along my own journey to reach that goal.

PROJECTION

I read phenomenologists Edmund Husserl, Maurice Merleau-Ponty, and Eugene Minkowski as a graduate student, and for me they offered framing and process for a practice I had been honing since early childhood: training mindful attention on a sentient being in hopes of glimpsing the lived experience of another. I did this first in grade school, moved by crushing boredom to fill the hours with friskier thoughts than our aging, deeply embittered teachers seemed able to inspire. A prime focus of my efforts was a fourth-grade friend. At recess she was warm and friendly, her bright blue eyes lighting up each time a new game was proposed. Yet in class she seemed to enter a persistently meditative state – her face blank, her breathing calm, and her dimpled hands resting still on her desk. If called upon, she had little to say. This sparked a curiosity about what she might be thinking, how those thoughts might feel, where they might lead. Surely not in the direction of my own unhelpful musings, stoked by my educator-mom's replies to complaints about the teacher and her lesson plan:

"Back then, teachers only needed two years of 'normal school' beyond high school," she explained. Then, after a meaningful pause, "Sometimes they never progressed any further."

My dad, never one for elaborate contextualization, was more direct. "That teacher's an old battle-ax," he summarized flatly.

Not surprisingly, my friend's experience of the classroom remained opaque to me. I didn't realize until later that there was no magic involved; I couldn't just stare and pretend to be her. I had to interact with my friend to learn why she was sitting so still and what it might mean.

Anthropologists do a lot of staring, though, and they are relatively skilled at describing what they see. As many have pointed out, however, ethnographic traditions privilege the visual at the expense of other senses and the cerebral at the expense of the visceral. However one chooses to navigate the theoretical outcroppings that have punctuated this debate for decades – and whether or not one's research methods involve explicit attention to the embodied self – contemporary ethnographers are fully aware that ontological understanding comes through participant observation as a sensory body engaged with a particular world at a particular time. Paul Stoller and Cheryl Olkes highlight this awareness in "The Taste of Ethnographic Things" (1989), an inspirational piece I first read at the suggestion of my colleague Erin Dean when we team-taught ethnographic methods. Stoller and Olkes cite this observation by Johannes Fabian: "As I see it now, the anthropologist and his interlocuters only 'know' when they meet each other in one and the same contemporality" (Fabian 1983 in Stoller and Olkes 1989, 26).

Fabian's *Time and the Other* has been an inspiration in my own writing, along with the work of both Vincent Crapanzano and Michael

Jackson. Jackson (1998, 98) takes up this concern in his discussion of whether and by what means one can "enter the world of another." He stresses that such understanding cannot be achieved intellectually, through what Alfred Schutz and others refer to as a "reciprocity of perspectives," but instead "must entail a psychophysical going beyond oneself in shared practical activity."

[margin note: I'm not sure what this means?]

Confined to the classroom and as yet unaware of such wisdom, I cast further for a way to "go beyond myself." In my childhood, dogs ran free until they were hit by cars or, in the rare notable instance, grew too old to do their business outside and had to be put to sleep. Gazing out the window, I would stare hard at a passing dog until I could project myself low to the ground, gathering scents on the path to the warm granite wall by the junior high, round the bend to the stores on Main Street. One cook was known to welcome canine customers in his busy luncheonette, so I might dip in there, crouched close to the scuffed hardwood floor, eager for scraps. Then on past several blocks of enticing sights and smells to a little hedge-lined park where all manner of dogs were free to mingle with their friends.

Projection in the Freudian sense is a cautionary term; it signals misrepresentation at best. In anthropology, projection has been linked to ethnocentrism, as in projecting one's own values and symbols onto others. "In one manifestation, it involves an inadequate but straightforward appeal to one's homegrown cultural experience in a foreign cultural context," writes Adam Etinson in his 2015 essay, "Some Myths about Ethnocentrism." "This can generate various errors," he points out. "Most typically, perhaps, it can blind us to the foreign features of an outside culture – via 'projection' – as when a traveler fails to realize that a swastika encountered in Tibet is, unlike at home, most likely not a symbol for Nazism."

[margin note: mentally & physically being in one's place?]

COMPASS

Fair enough, but there are other kinds of projections. "[T]o extend outward beyond a usual point" is among the definitions offered by Merriam-Webster for the verb *project*. This source explains that the word can be traced to the Latin for "to throw forward," and it is the promise, potential, and danger of this concept I would like to explore.

(margin handwriting: "In what ways can ethnographic distortion?")

Any map is a projection, for instance, an effort to represent three dimensions in two. It's a bold distortion but a fully acknowledged one, a visual tool applied to both perception and navigation. In *Four Master Tropes,* literary critic Kenneth Burke uses maps as an example when he suggests, "For metonymy we could substitute reduction" (1969, 503). He sees metonymy and "its partner, reduction" as respective devices of poetic and scientific realism (1969, 506). Further, he guides readers to note that "a reduction is a *representation.* If I reduce the contours of the United States, for instance, to the terms of a relief map, I have within these limits 'represented' the United States" (1969, 507, emphasis in original). Burke's discussion of tropes is related to his analysis of "degrees of being" in dramatic characters: how vivid and deep they are depends on the overlaying of literary devices to create characters who can be approached and examined from multiple perspectives.

In another effort to get at the complexities of writing's impact, Yunte Huang (2002, 2, 4) identifies "three textual means by which the imaging of the Other's cultural reality may be attempted: ethnography, translation, and intertextual travel." He talks about how readers see the unknown world without really "being there" in Geertz's sense, through "a process in which multiple versions of the original are reduced to a version that foregrounds the translator's own agenda."

Good ethnographies and the vivid historical representations that make best-seller lists share many challenges, in part because they demand of the writers an imaginative projection, a map across time and place – a need to walk where their subjects walked, touch what they handled, meet the sun at a particular time of day. Once there, writers must dare to reach beyond the etic for sustained engagement with the embodied sensory realities of these others. The bridge to this awareness is always makeshift and incomplete, but in strong works the evidence of bricolage melts away and readers are swept up in a narrative they can experience as seamless and immediate, a sensorial gestalt.

CANVAS

Multimodal comparisons can be productive in helping to understand the reaching and bridging needed to make one's subjects "walk and talk," as Stephen King would say. Robbin Legere Henderson's drawings for the book *Immigrant Girl, Radical Woman* provide an outstanding example. The text is a memoir of early feminism and labor organizing left by Henderson's grandmother, Matilda Rabinowitz. The author's descriptions of her various environments are vivid, but the light and movement Henderson captures in her drawings take the story further. The shadows on buildings and faces are imagined but not generic; they are the real light she recorded with an artist's eye by visiting many of the locations where her grandmother had lived. The artistic and anthropological result is multiple mise-en-scènes. In her preface to the book, she writes that "my travels to many of the places mentioned in Matilda's memoir, especially those places where Matilda struggled to improve labor conditions, help me imagine her…. They help me see some of the landscape that was the background to her life, and I feel her presence" (Henderson 2017). The reader does as well. Another example is Alisse Waterston's work for *My Father's Wars* (2014), where she mines geographic and social byways in Poland, Cuba, and Puerto Rico in a vividly engaging effort to situate and narrate her father's story.

Anthropologists might break some traditional rules to attempt this kind of representation, but it is already happening all around and permeating the way life is experienced and apprehended. Matilda Rabinowitz wrote her memoir in an era when the printed page had little competition. Yes, there was radio and film, and television was coming along. But today's intertextual travel proceeds on an ever-expanding range of platforms.

"The idea that the medium is the message increasingly will be passé," declared State of the News Media 2004, the Pew Research Center's widely respected, ongoing research project that tracks trends in print and broadcast journalism. "This is an exciting possibility that offers the potential of new audiences, new ways of storytelling, more immediacy and more citizen involvement." The statement was certainly prescient, but the speed and dimensions of the change are dazzling. Consider, for example, the record-breaking audiences for broadcast coverage of the first 2016 presidential debate, with an estimated 84 million viewers logged by Nielson for live coverage by 13 networks. Nielson also marked "17.1 million Twitter interactions from 2.7 million people in the US related to the debate on Monday, Sept. 26, 2016." According to Nielson's findings from 2014, however, this need not signal competition between television and the internet.

[handwritten margin notes: "# putting you in that place", "Intertextual traveling"]

"Eighty-four percent of smartphone and tablet owners say they use their devices as second-screens while watching TV at the same time," Nielson reported. "Consumers use second screens to deepen their engagement with what they're watching, including activities such as looking up information about the characters and plot lines, or researching and purchasing products and services advertised. One of the more popular second-screen activities is using social TV: roughly one million Americans turn to Twitter to discuss TV on an average day," Nielson found in 2014. Phrases such as "social TV" and "second-screen companion" have signaled an ongoing shift in how news is consumed, shared, and, one assumes, understood. According to Tracy McGraw, summing up the pandemic year on Twitter Insights, "Globally, there were the equivalent of more than 7,000 Tweets per minute about TV and movies" in 2020.

Internet communication in its ever-expanding forms has blurred the line between journalism as a source of institutionally vetted information and myriad "takes" on the world, mediated only by the individual's perspective.

Internet communication in its ever-expanding forms has blurred the line between journalism as a source of institutionally vetted information and myriad "takes" on the world, mediated only by the individual's perspective.

Yet organized journalism, albeit leaner and perhaps meaner, certainly remains in the business of communicating what David Altheide and Robert Snow have identified as journalists' primary charge, "to communicate the complexities and ambiguities of 'real world' conditions" (Altheide and Snow 1991, 51). Substitute anthropology for journalism and ethnography for television, and anthropologists will recognize a common direction. After an era of confusion and uncertainty, the value-added potential of multimodal, multi-platform storytelling is becoming increasingly clear.

Anthropologists are still transfixed by the raw immediacy of the internet, however. As a group, they have yet to appreciate the associated danger to what they do best – spending time with people in their daily lives. Once free-ranging reporters, who now spend much of their workday tethered to computers in harshly lit newsrooms, understand how "thin" the description has become. The more frantically occupied one is with the task of retrieving information collected by other, remote sources, the less time remains for the firsthand encounter, the fresh take, the news in the true sense of "new."

Journalists were once ridiculed and excoriated for being too eager, too much on the scene, making pests of themselves in a bird-dog effort to get the "scoop." These days they are criticized for being too remote, too intellectually and viscerally removed from current events. ⌐Bit by bit, they have traded away the primacy and privilege of the extended, eye-witness account of community life.⌐ *Will this happen to Anth. Why or why not?*

As a group, anthropologists have yet to appreciate the associated danger to what they do best – spending time with people in their daily lives.... The more frantically occupied one is with the task of retrieving information collected by other, remote sources, the less time remains for the firsthand encounter, the fresh take, the news in the true sense of "new."

Contemporary ethnographers taste the journalists' frustration; it is not so easy to compete for privileged vantage points with whole television networks devoted exclusively to travel and cross-cultural exploration. "The dreams of television at its birth were already global," Richard Dienst reminds his readers in *Still Life in Real Time*. "On the basis of the most rudimentary experiments in image transmission, ⌐televisuality was immediately imagined as an all-encompassing putting-into-view of the world" (Dienst 1994)⌐

Dienst writes compellingly about how telecommunication has brought about what I regard, with a bow to Marx, as a⌐universe of temporal substitution⌐ Television news stories are juxtaposed in such a heterotypic way – disaster in Indonesia follows unrest in the Middle East follows bomb scare in London – that all trouble on such a mass scale becomes oddly equidistant. At the same time, burglary follows murder follows carjacking on the local scene, amplifying the notion that victims are infinitely substitutable and fueling community distrust. Add a remote control and an embedded recording device, and the temporal/historical dimension becomes just as interchangeable as content. *It's a Wonderful Life* is substituted for the evening news, a 1950s-era sitcom, a rebroadcast of *Saturday Night Live* from 1980, a football game in progress, Buster Keaton chased by a train, Sylvester in perpetual pursuit of Tweetie Pie. And as more consumers turn to online sources for news, merchandise, and entertainment, boundaries of chronology, context, and source are further blurred. Bloggers, RSS feeds, and other aggregators cull stories from a range of sources and repackage them. From a consumer's perspective, then,⌐one story can indeed be substituted for the next, and at the same time⌐ the experience presents a gestalt that is new, vivid, and temporally immediate.

The idea that people are no longer their own. Stories + people are no longer their own.

In what ways can this change in a traditional academic setting?

So don't stuff your message in a bottle and cast it into that pond where academic publications bob serenely, hoping someday to be read. Study your narrative with a critical eye, make it leaner, and share drafts with like-minded folks who are headed in your general direction. Then time to let it go – not too much time, mind you – into that media sea where outcomes are always unpredictable and sometimes downright scary. Worth it, though, because the chances are so much greater that it will be read and understood by anyone who finds it.

SUMMARY

Get a grip on style. Crafting a compelling narrative is part of the social historian's skill set, but most other nonfiction writers in the social sciences chose writing from the add-on menu, if at all. It's never too late to order up something, though. There are many writing courses and workshops available, both on and off campus and online. Ask around to find one that meets your budget and your needs. For free you can start or join an informal writing group – this really helps. Be explicit about your individual and collective goals, monitor both rigorously, meet monthly at the minimum and require text-sharing among all members.

Most of all, trim the junk reading and focus your attention on the writing you most admire. Figure out what makes it "walk and talk," then try those strategies in your own work.

Mind the urgency/relevance twins. Timeliness and relevance are rarely found alone in popular media. No matter how hard-won or rare information might be, it must also be current. New data is foregrounded in narratives about contemporary issues, expertise is background. Reversing that order yields a wordy opinion piece at best. Know the difference between information, which is a kind of currency, and expertise, which has intangible but negotiable value. Attempting to weigh in as an "expert" with work conducted years ago might fit on the op-ed page, but only if one steps up within days or even hours of the news event in question. Be aware that most anthropological data won't pass as news, particularly if the subjects' names and locations must remain confidential.

If you have fresh field knowledge to share with a mainstream publication, write a short summary, do the research to find an appropriate editor and contact that person immediately, asking to hear back within

idea of urgency + research

two days. Write again after 24 hours, wait that second day, then move on. If your platform is a personal blog or post, meaning quality control rests solely in your hands, the same urgency/relevance pairing applies.

Go full-on multimodal. There is no substitute for substance; bedazzling folks with one's technical skills might be easy, but it is just as easily called out. Choices to integrate text with sound, photography, video, graphic arts, social media, interactive technologies, and more must be made with deliberation and care, but the good news is that graduate-level training in digital storytelling is available and the impact of well-crafted pieces can be profound.

Harness jargon to your own ends. Some might argue that jargon should be foresworn completely, but I disagree. Any chance to share anthropological viewpoints should be taken, but these sometimes require theoretical framing. Learning a new term or two is a good thing and I credit readers with curiosity and intelligence. The problem comes when writers don't know how to explain their ideas, and jargon provides a conveniently intimidating screen. That's lazy, not scholarly. Be sure you know what you're talking about, then proceed with confidence.

Dare to be vulnerable. Academics are a cautious lot when it comes to writing, resulting in a naive defensiveness that serves no one well. Today, however, social media gives the average person a sense of the damage critics can do when they don't like a writer's style or subject matter or point of view. It's painful, something journalists have known for generations. And yet they persist because they believe that silence is unacceptable, an abdication of responsibility – dangerous, even. Increasingly, anthropologists are coming to feel the same, empowering them to speak out and to support each other in the process, as journalists do. So, as I have said before, dance to the edge. Take a chance.

FOR DISCUSSION

1 Anthropologists have long been criticized for jargon-filled, unintelligible writing; however, using jargon can also be seen as crediting readers with curiosity and intelligence. How do you know when to edit jargon or when to keep relevant anthropological concepts in your public writing?

2 Engaging in public writing can be intimidating, but it is important to take a chance. Having a strong network of support improves your writing and provides an opportunity to better understand your own work through others' perspectives. In which ways might you support colleagues who are concerned about the feedback they might receive from critics?

3 New data is foregrounded in journalistic narratives about contemporary issues, expertise is background. How might you quickly update your research in order to properly address a contemporary issue?

4 Interactive technologies can be useful in the creation of public work, but they should not substitute for substance. Which technical skills would be useful to hone for your project, and at what point should you focus on your own anthropological skill set and recruit strategic collaborators to help you tell your story?

REFERENCES

Altheide, David, and Robert Snow. 1991. *Media Worlds in the Postjournalism Era.* New York: Aldine de Gruyter.

Bonilla, Yarimar, Elizabeth Chin, Dána-Ain Davis, Antoinette Jackson, and Gina Ulysse. 2014. "Reflections on Kara Walker's 'a Subtlety, or the Marvelous Sugar Baby.'" *Anthropology Now,* July 24. http://anthronow.com/reach/reflections-on-kara-walkers-a-subtlety-or-the-marvelous-sugar-baby.

Burke, Kenneth. 1969. "Four Master Tropes." In *A Grammar of Motives.* Berkeley: University of California Press.

Dienst, Richard. 1994. *Still Life in Real Time: Theory After Television.* Durham: Duke University Press.

Etinson, Adam. 2018. "Some Myths about Ethnocentrism." *Australasian Journal of Philosophy* 96, no. 2. https://doi.org/10.1080/00048402.2017.1343363.

Fabian, Johannes. 1983. *Time and the Other: How Anthropology Makes Its Object.* New York: Columbia University Press.

Grindal, Bruce, and Robin Rhodes. 1987. "Journalism and Anthropology Share Several Similarities." *Journalism Educator* 41, no. 4: 4, 11–13, 33.

Hale, Constance. 2013. *Sin and Syntax: How to Craft Wicked Good Prose.* New York: Three Rivers Press.

Henderson, Robbin Legere. 2017. *Immigrant Girl, Radical Woman.* Ithaca: Cornell University Press.

Jackson, Michael. 1998. *Minima Ethnographica: Intersubjectivity and the Anthropological Project.* Chicago: University of Chicago Press.

McGraw, Tracy. "Spending 2020 Together on Twitter." https://blog.twitter.com/en_us/authors.traylove23.

Nielson Insights. 2014. "What's Empowering the New Digital Consumer?" February 10. https://www.nielsen.com/us/en/insights/article/2014/whats-empowering-the-new-digital-consumer/.

Nielson Insights. 2016. "First Presidential Debate of 2016 Draws 84 Million Viewers." September 27. https://www.nielsen.com/us/en/insights/article/2016/first-presidential-debate-of-2016-draws-84-million-viewers/.

Project for Excellence in Journalism. 2004. "State of the News Media 2004." Pew Research Center. https://assets.pewresearch.org/wp-content/uploads/sites/13/2017/05/24141554/State-of-the-News-Media-Report-2004-FINAL.pdf.

Stoller, Paul, and Cheryl Olkes. 1989. "The Taste of Ethnographic Things." In *The Taste of Ethnographic Things: The Senses in Ethnography.* Philadelphia: University of Pennsylvania Press.

Vesperi, Maria D. 2011. "Taking Chances." In *Anthropology off the Shelf: Anthropologists on Writing,* ed. Alisse Waterston and Maria D. Vesperi. Malden: Wiley-Blackwell.

Waterston, Alisse. 2014. *My Father's Wars: Migration, Memory and the Violence of a Century.* New York: Routledge.

PART TWO

The World Wide Web

CHAPTER FOUR

Cool Enough to Make a Difference

Daniel H. Lende

STORY #1

Start in the middle, writing guides say. In December of 2007, Greg Downey and I established the *Neuroanthropology* blog. We had been colleagues in the Department of Anthropology at the University of Notre Dame, our offices next to each other, and had talked about how cognitive science and neuroscience helped illuminate topics we researched during our respective fieldwork in Colombia and Brazil. Then, Greg took a position across the globe, following love and adventure to Macquarie University in Sydney, Australia.

We decided to use neuroanthropology.net as a way to continue our conversations. Distance forced us. At that point, blogging was still relatively new, and we were inspired by blogs such as *Savage Minds* (now *Anthro {Dendrum}*), which had begun to explore the academic possibilities of online engagement. We were also intrigued by how we could use blogging to do something more formal than just talk. Little did we realize the impact that having our conversations in public would make.

The blog grew quickly, from a few hundred views the first month to consistently gathering 20,000 or 30,000 views per month later in 2008. Suddenly we had an audience, and it wasn't just other anthropologists.

All manner of people came to read what we wrote – neuroscientists, psychologists, journalists, people looking for specific information on topics, and students from a range of disciplines. And the audience wasn't just in the United States and Australia – the blog had a global reach. At the height of its success, people from more than 200 countries and territories would access the blog during any particular year.

We did use the blog to build neuroanthropology as a new approach within anthropology. The blog let us explore literature, develop initial ideas, and see what worked and what didn't. By putting stuff "out there," we got a type of immediate peer feedback that we would not have gotten otherwise. Moreover, we interacted with people outside our disciplinary envelope, learning from clinicians, bench scientists, people who suffered from particular disorders, and more. Those interactions helped us to develop a more robust, interdisciplinary approach. This online scholarship buttressed our other efforts, such as organizing conference sessions and hosting a stand-alone conference on neuroanthropology that later became *The Encultured Brain: An Introduction to Neuroanthropology* (2012), published with MIT Press.

The blog also developed into something more than just a way to expand how we did our scholarship. We gained a public voice that we wouldn't have had if we had just done academic scholarship. We could comment on current events and controversies in the field, and we could have posts that were fun and others that were serious. We learned that not everything we posted had to technically be "neuroanthropology"; we controlled the content we posted, and that opened the range of what we could do. In that sense, the *Neuroanthropology* blog was something separate from neuroanthropology as scholarship. The blog operated more as a brand, a place where people could come to read human interest stories, critical takes, and defenses of human diversity.

For me personally, this side of blogging mattered as much as building the scholarship. I liked having a voice! In graduate school, I had written in similar ways, writing notes and commentaries, typing up pages and pages that just sat there in my computer files. I saw it then as a way to help me learn and to generate notes for future reference. Then I started blogging. It was similar, just now I was doing it in public. No longer ideas for myself, but engaging a public electric. That brought changes – I aimed to write better and I took advantage of the possibilities offered by the internet. But the process of writing, in many ways, wasn't that different. I reviewed content, wrote notes in the margin or on a piece of paper, and then wrote. Just now I added more polish and aimed for a more coherent order for the final post. I quickly saw how blogging mattered for academia. Students at Notre Dame helped me to realize this.

As I taught my classes, I saw them going online to find information and ideas. They checked their phones or computers before they went to the library. They got their news by whatever Google told them was relevant. And they started working on papers using online sources. For me, the overarching lesson was clear – if anthropology wasn't there online, then it wouldn't exist for students. For me, then, it became a moral imperative to add to anthropology's presence online.

For me, the overarching lesson was clear – if anthropology wasn't there online, then it wouldn't exist for students. For me, then, it became a moral imperative to add to anthropology's presence online.

Creating an online portal for conveying anthropology brought other lessons. Blogging wasn't like teaching, where I had a given authority by being at the front of the classroom. Online, reputation has to be earned, and given how many types of content are available online, reputation is central to building a presence. Students have to come back to the class. Readers have to decide to come back.

Speed mattered. Links mattered. Images mattered. But so too did high-quality content. And if that long-form work took longer to create, that was fine – it helped establish what we were about at *Neuroanthropology*.

Over time, I learned a lot about how to get on that first page of Google search results, such as having an informative rather than an evocative title, linking to related material, and making sure the topic of the post was mentioned up front, all to match how Google's bots and algorithms worked.

Good writing made a difference, too. I came up with a general format for posts, one that I had students follow when they created group blog posts as part of class projects. This writing strategy was adapted to what worked online:

1 a good hook up front, something to catch people's attention;
2 this would be followed by a summary statement about what the post would do, because you need to give readers a reason to keep reading;

3   then a series of points made with short paragraphs, because people
    tend to jump over large blocks of text online;
4   finally, for readers who make it to the end, some sort of pay-off,
    something fun or a new avenue to explore or additional resources.

I also realized how much curation matters online. So much stuff online
was just one-time commentary; sites that brought together high-quality
material were rarer. Curation, in fact, was one of the main routes to reputation. Too few sites do this sort of work, but it is an absolute necessity
for building an audience online. In one form or another, curation creates success – a good stable of authors, an assessment of current events,
a consideration of central sources, and so forth.

I became skilled at doing my "Wednesday Round Up," a quick overview of scholarly articles, news stories, science writing, and other blog
posts that struck me as important to the broad themes covered by
Neuroanthropology as a blog. Taking the time to write quick takes on a
high-quality selection out of the deluge of content that gets created
every week – people liked that. I also did this sort of curation with significant events: from the American Anthropological Association's view on
science, to Florida's governor, Rick Scott, saying the state didn't need
more anthropologists, to Sandy Hook and the massacre of children
and debates over guns, mental health, and violence. Curation, effective
writing, and taking advantage of the multimedia possibilities of the internet all helped the *Neuroanthropology* blog build success. But I learned
that there were two other demands that come with creating a robust
online presence. One is simply creating enough content so that people
come on a regular basis, to check whether there is something new or
via search engines that help to guide people to one's site. That level of
speed – daily or weekly or monthly
content – is often at odds with the
slower pace of academic life, where
an article might take months to write
and a book, years.

That level of speed – daily or weekly or monthly content – is often at odds with the slower pace of academic life, where an article might take months to write and a book, years.

The other demand is the need
to move beyond one's own exper-
tise, a scholar's specific area of research that represents years of effort and learning. Online, people didn't want to hear me talk about
how everything relates back to addiction and Colombia and the

intersection of brain and culture. Sure, I had many posts related to my own interests. But I learned that many readers just want a different take, something that doesn't come from the typical pundits or represent business as usual. Anthropology offers that different take in spades. And people like the types of answers that anthropology offers. Becoming more of a generalist is something that helps to foster the creation of good material that appeals to a broader range of people.

I learned how to draw on my holistic training, critical thinking, ability to grasp others' points of view, and understanding of field research as I crafted responses to broad scholarly debates, advances in science, current controversies, and breaking news. Readers wanted more anthropology, not just neuroanthropology.

STORY #2

Blogging has provided the most visible public impact during my career. But my cool anthropology started earlier than that, through a combination of mistakes and realizations that pushed me in new directions. Before I started graduate school, I spent three years in Bogotá, Colombia as a counselor to adolescents who had drug problems. I also worked as a freelance journalist. Then, in graduate school, I was trained to develop exacting research designs, get grants and publish, and pursue tenure-track jobs. For my doctoral dissertation, I did mixed-methods research back in Colombia, building a biocultural approach to addiction. When I graduated, I went back to Colombia to tell the treatment center all that I had learned. I used lots of technical and academic details, just as if I were on a job talk.

It fell on deaf ears. Don't get me wrong. The assembled crowd – therapists, parents, residents in the treatment program – listened. But I hadn't offered them much of use. I didn't know how. I had been trained in executing the highest level of research. I hadn't been trained in having an impact. Even the most informed research might not be useful to the public if I am not clearly connecting the dots on how to apply my findings.

It took me time to realize what I needed to do. Originally I thought, magically, that studying addiction as a researcher would lead directly to applicable results – if somehow I understood the problem well enough, I would be able to solve it. But it was not that simple. I saw that basic science research was important. But it was not enough if one's goal was to do something more.

Today I teach students to do both "about" and "how-to" research. Get data about the problem, that classic sort of scholarship. But also get data that directly relates to applied impacts. In my case, to get data not just to understand addiction, but to understand how to do something about it. Both types of knowledge are important.

As field-based researchers, anthropologists in particular need to be data-driven. First, we often can't go back to research what makes a difference. And as ethnographers using inductive approaches, we need data to help us think through what might help or not.

Too often we focus on figuring out culture, inequality, positionality, and all the rest, but we don't use our same methodological approaches to develop robust answers about what can make a difference in people's lives.

Too often we focus on figuring out culture, inequality, positionality, and all the rest, but we don't use our same methodological approaches to develop robust answers about what can make a difference in people's lives.

We also need to learn how to translate our results in ways that can have an impact. Applied data is a start, but there is still not a direct line from research to change. Translational models, applied theories, and how-to and practical knowledge all matter. For example, one's research can show that specific policy changes are needed, but creating actual policy takes skills, relationships, and knowledge that generally lies outside academia, not inside it.

Finally, as researchers, we need to consider early on what might be useful to the people with whom we work. For my doctoral work, I developed research for solely academic purposes. I did that well. And then I fell flat on my face when I tried to give back. Today, I make sure my students not only ask but can answer questions that matter:

- What are your applied outcomes?
- What will be useful to your community partners, not just to you?
- How will you make a difference for them?
- How are you incorporating these considerations into your research design?

These questions become part of developing a cooler research design before any data collection has taken place.

I learned to do these things – data, translation, and applied outcomes – by engaging. When I became a tenure-track professor at the University of Notre Dame, I became involved with the Center for Social Concerns there. The center integrated Catholic teachings with academic efforts; its work resonated with the Catholic institutions I knew in Colombia, helping others via both ministry and scholarship. The center in particular advocated for community-based research, which develops research with community partners. In other words, the research design, including the research problem itself, comes out of collaboration. Community-based participatory research (CBPR), as it is often called now, provides a strong framework for anthropologists who are interested in combining qualitative approaches with applied impacts. But it can work for many types of research, and it often starts by asking community partners: What are your problems that you'd like to know something more about? What can we help you with?

But I learned these lessons the hard way. I still remember one of the first projects I did, where undergraduate students and I worked with a local partner to address health issues related to access to health and counseling services for HIV/AIDS. We did the semester-long project and turned in a comprehensive 25-page report to our community partner. It was dense with data and complete with citations. I was proud of what the students were able to produce in a semester, and I knew other professors would be impressed.

I gave the director the report. She took it, felt its heft, looked at the title and then the opening pages. And then she tried very hard as she said to me, "That's nice."

There was little in the report that she could use. All this work, and we hadn't got the right data, figured out how to translate it, or deliver concrete outcomes to our partner.

But I learned. And that learning often required listening. Interesting problems can come from anywhere. For the second time around, on a health project related to breast cancer services in South Bend, I met with my partner in her office, and we just talked. I asked her about her work, and what was going on, and what she would like to know more about.

She spoke about a recent counseling session that became something more. Instead of reviewing standard health practices, she and the other breast cancer survivors started talking about all the humorous things that had come as part of their journey. And instead of an hour session, she said, they spent three hours talking. And so our research project on humor and breast cancer was born. We learned that humor was an important coping mechanism for women, and that sharing stories made humor work, and that humor grew in importance as a way for women to process what had happened to them, particularly after the initial shocks of diagnosis and early rounds of treatment. And we collected these women's stories into a colorful book designed for use in clinical settings, and that became the centerpiece for a large fundraising gala.

That ripple of effects all came from listening and opening oneself to the possibilities of combining research and impact.

STORY #3

I have paid a price for being cool, for following what I saw as making a difference versus what often "counts" in academic settings. That is the third story, to work to be the difference, not just for me but for others who might want to try similar things. My promotions have not been as easy as some of my colleagues; I often have felt that I have to work double, to do both academic and engaged stuff; and I haven't got as much credit as I would like for what I see as valuable work. But rather than complain, I have found ways to try to create changes, small as they might be, that can help others.

I have worked with my own department and with the American Anthropological Association (AAA) to expand the scope of scholarship. Within the department, it was important to not just have a vision statement – yes, we value these other ways of doing research and having an impact – but to make sure the criteria used for evaluation and the examples given explicitly recognized a broader range of outcomes than just books, journal articles, chapters, and academic reports. Similarly, for the AAA, I provided input so that the largest organization of professional anthropologists in the world also says these types of outcomes matter, providing legitimacy to people who want to do something other than academia as usual.

I also took up an offered position on the AAA's Publishing Futures Committee, which offers guidance and feedback on the direction of

AAA journals. Here, working on sustainability, creating greater access, and expanding the quality and impact of journals forms the behind-the-scenes work that supports what others do. For some AAA journals, that means open access, for others it means finding digital means of adding more voices to what they do, and for others it is continuing to speak to their core group of scholars even as digital technology has transformed publishing.

As I relayed previously, I have also worked hard to incorporate the lessons I have learned about applied and public work into my teaching, to guide and instruct coming generations on how they might find ways to make a difference.

Teaching is our most consistent access to an audience beyond anthropology. Teaching is where the university intersects with people who will then go on to have careers other than being a professor or researcher.

I have come to realize that teaching is our underappreciated way of having an impact. Teaching is our most consistent access to an audience beyond anthropology. Teaching is where the university intersects with people who will then go on to have careers other than being a professor or researcher.

And teaching provides the most effective way for others to not have to repeat the mistakes I have made. They will surely make their own mistakes, and hopefully learn from them, but my students start further down the engaged road. Teaching offers something more as well. Teaching is where we as academics most explicitly practice the things that can make a difference outside the university. We deal with students on a daily basis who want to learn but might not have the background and training that our colleagues do. We have to lecture on topics on which we are not experts but still need to say something substantive. We need to meet students where they are, not where we would like them to be. We have to use not just words and theories, but persuasion, images and videos, and specific techniques, from how we arrange lectures to the ways we structure assignments to how we teach a topic in sequential fashion. All these things are exactly what can help us have an impact outside the academy. We just have to better translate what we already know how to do as teachers and then plan and execute for the specific types of outcomes and audiences we want to reach. After that, we can learn from feedback and mistakes and what works and what doesn't to make improvements.

To begin to do this type of public work, academics need space and support so we can engage and learn. Universities should encourage the public engagement of scholars, just as they support our work in the classroom. Doing this sort of work should count as much as teaching, as research, as service, depending on what a specific person is doing. And just as there are now instructors who specialize in teaching, so too universities should have scholars whose jobs focus on public engagement.

Universities often think that the fruits of their labors will sell themselves. But in a world where attention and money flows along digital lines, the classic model of research and teaching is not enough. Ideas don't win out on their own. If universities don't engage in public arenas, then they will not do as well in places where expertise, authority, and credentials no longer carry the weight they once did. It is not enough for the marketing team to push news; faculty and students themselves should have the support, financially and technologically and institutionally, to do the work that will help our ideas come to life not just in libraries and in classrooms but in the many media we now use to communicate, share, and debate.

WHAT COMES AHEAD

The legacy of the *Neuroanthropology* blog stands. Over 1,000 posts. More than 6 million views, with a monthly core audience of more than 20,000 people at the height of its success. A wide range of authors – colleagues and students – who learned from this type of writing and engagement. And scholarly publications in journals such as *American Anthropologist* and *Annals of Anthropological Practice*.

But I no longer blog as I once did, confining myself to microblogging and curating materials on Facebook, an occasional tweet, and a guest post here or there. And it is because I am one person.

It took me time to learn that I had one shot a day of good writing. And if I spent that writing effort on the blog, then I couldn't work as well on the book I was starting to write. I wanted that book to convey my in-depth scholarship on addiction, but in a different way, bringing together the many lessons I have learned along the way – to aim for a broader audience, to include public impacts, and to read well.

I cannot do it all. I miss the direct engagement of community-based approaches and the immediacy of blogging. But this book is another step in a journey to help broaden what I and others can do as academics.

So, to close, a cascade.

There are many forms to engage, which this volume on "cool" anthropology so amply demonstrates. And it can start by aiming to increase the impact of your own research. It doesn't need to sit only in a journal or a book. An exhibit, a YouTube video, a blog post, a public lecture, concrete outcomes for specific communities, and so on – there are many ways that scholars can expand how they engage. And it is clear that doing this actually results in both better scholarship and in more citations. Multiple audiences bring multiple forms of review and exposure to new ideas and approaches, thus improving research. And presentations in varied formats provide access to a wider range of people, most of them outside of your discipline (or just coming into a discipline), and suddenly, they want to build on your work and to incorporate it into what they are doing.

Public impact can also go beyond one's own research. There is tremendous interest out there in questions about human diversity, well-being, cross-cultural encounters, and so forth. These intersect with big public questions about issues like migration, the impact of technology, how to handle climate change, and addressing violence of all sorts. But academic viewpoints are often not there in these debates. Even if an academic shows up, it is generally not one who brings the critical and global perspectives that come with anthropology. We need more anthropology out there, both online and in robust public debate, providing data and viewpoints as people seek to address questions about this life and world of ours.

Anthropologists can also act in a more local way. One of the powers of anthropology is our ability to connect, to listen, to move between social spaces, to engage with multiple actors. Our modern institutions, companies and governments and other bureaucracies, are not built to create connections and communities. Anthropologists are excellent mediators, with the ability to speak with both those in power and those who are marginalized, and engage in exchange and communication that can create flows that cut across our modern bureaucracies. We can bring some organic solidarity, some *communitas*, in ways that defy the ideologies and exclusions that mark so many social spaces.

Our modern institutions, companies and governments and other bureaucracies, are not built to create connections and communities. Anthropologists are excellent mediators, with the ability to speak with both those in power and those who are marginalized, and engage in exchange and communication that can create flows that cut across our modern bureaucracies.

Finally, we can exercise our creativity. We can make art that intersects with our scholarship, we can write in ways that draw on techniques from fiction and nonfiction, we can create exhibits that meld ideas and engagement, we can podcast and YouTube in ways that are funny and immersive. We can develop the field not just as the most humanistic but also the most expressive of the social sciences.

As anthropologists, we can imagine. We can think globally and connect locally. We can write specifically and engage holistically. We can investigate in depth and throw ourselves out of our academic depths. And when we do these things, we learn first that we can have a greater impact than we may have imagined. Then, we learn how to have an even greater impact.

FOR DISCUSSION

1 Public engagement is scholarship, and getting anthropology out to diverse publics impacts public discourse. What are some tangible and intangible ways the anthropological perspective can affect broad public conversations about important societal issues?

2 Research alone does not provide all the answers. What considerations beyond conducting/publishing research could be helpful in developing practical how-to approaches in problem solving for public issues?

3 It is in the spirit of anthropological ethics to work on problems that are relevant to specific communities. What are some of the pros and cons to beginning a project with your own curiosities versus the idea coming directly from the community?

4 Institutional support deeply impacts what work we do and how we do it. What are some ways we can invest

in institutional change alongside our own individual efforts?

5 As anthropologists, our focus is often on very specific communities and theoretical frameworks. Public engagement allows us to be more creative and move beyond our own research and disciplinary constraints. How far can we take this creativity and still call it scholarship?

REFERENCE

Lende, D.H., and G. Downey, eds. 2012. *The Encultured Brain: An Introduction to Neuroanthropology*. Cambridge: MIT Press.

CHAPTER FIVE

PopAnth: The Conversation

*Erin B. Taylor, John McCreery, and Gwendolen Lynch
with Laura Miller, Elizabeth Challinor, and Celia Emmelhainz*

In 2012, during a conversation in Erin's PopAnth group on the *Open Anthropology Cooperative* (OAC) website, Greg Downey made the point that "[we've] talked a lot about this, but I'm not 100% convinced that talking about it helps. I think we have to practice DOING accessible, popular writing and see what works." That call to arms inspired Gwendolen Lynch and Erin Taylor to found the *PopAnth* website. It was envisaged as a platform to publish anthropologists' popular writing, to help each other figure out what popular anthropology can be, and to discover how to produce it.

PopAnth was, and still is, an experiment. We "let a thousand flowers bloom," allowing authors to explore a wide range of topics, from toilet brushes to pens marketed to women, from the material culture of World War II trenches to ghost bikes. We were curious to see what floated to the surface; what stories were hiding in the minds of our fellow anthropologists that wouldn't make the cut for academic publication.

PopAnth describes itself as presenting anthropological discoveries – too often left buried in academic journals – in a popular format. We hope that readers respond, "Wow, I didn't know that." Since we began,

PopAnth has published 144 articles by 74 authors in four categories that roughly correspond to the "four fields" approach: "Archaeology," "Contemporary Culture," "Language and Communication," and "The Human Body." Some articles were read by hundreds of thousands of readers. But we never asked ourselves seriously, "What makes this worth knowing?" Lack of focus may or may not have been a problem. Our opinions differ.

The chapter is written as a conversation between three of the founders of *PopAnth* – Gwendolen, Erin, and John – with some additions by our fourth founder, Liz Challinor, and two of our main editors, Laura Miller and Celia Emmelhainz. We chose this format to highlight the multiple meanings and purposes *PopAnth* has for each of us and to avoid merging our analysis into a single perspective. What emerges is a conversation in which *PopAnth* is a protagonist. The lessons we learned, and our interpretations of them, have much to say about the role that popular anthropology can play in general.

US

Erin

I am a reformed academic. I run a small business called Finthropology that provides insights into people's financial behavior. Since I have long been averse to narrowing down my professional focus to one specific topic, reaching this point was a complex process. Desire led me to anthropology. It was the idea of fieldwork that first grabbed me, but it was the discipline's broad focus on "the study of humankind in all times and places" (Haviland et al. 2013) that kept me there. Above all, reading anthropology showed me that anything can be the subject of analysis. I wanted to produce this kind of writing myself and help other people to see what I saw.

I went on to do a PhD at the University of Sydney and wrote my own blog while doing fieldwork. Throughout my postdoc at the University of Lisbon, I continued my popular writing. Rather than pump out as much academic content as possible, I allocated time to writing for a wider audience.

Gwendolen

I am a reformed technologist. For a couple of decades, I worked as a business systems architect dealing with the intersection of infrastructure and human culture, globally. In 2011, when I began working with academic anthropologists, it concerned me that the discipline was underrepresented in science communication.

To me, it was obvious that broader communication of the knowledge gathered by academic ethnographers can be a valuable tool in assisting members of the general public to understand "differences" and the (cultural) reasoning behind them. It can help to counter and tear down flawed assumptions, such as humans are rational actors, and others created by misinformation, which in turn potentially culminate in dangerous polarizations. However, broader dissemination of this knowledge requires platforms that give authors visibility, and support to shape writing for a wider audience.

One painfully obvious impediment was that for academics, balancing workloads – admin, teaching, research – has become increasingly difficult. Research funds are shrinking while institutional pressure is increasing, and knowledge production is undervalued. The incentive to be a science communicator tends to be minimal as a result. So this raised the practical question of how to better support this community to communicate beyond its academic boundaries.

John

I am a failed academic. I didn't get tenure. Following my wife, a PhD candidate in Japanese literature, to Japan, I found a job that became a stepping stone to 13 years as an English-language copywriter for Japan's second-largest advertising agency.

Working in the Japanese advertising industry during the late 1980s economic bubble was a lot of fun. The mortification of not getting tenure had faded, and my academic itch revived.

I wrote an article with the cheeky title "Why Don't We See Some Real Money Here?" It was published by the *Journal of Chinese Religions* in 1990. Then I wrote "Negotiating with Demons: The Uses of Magical Language."

I had, however, failed to cite any research done in the previous decade. A new thing called the internet made it easy to learn who should have been cited, rewrite and resubmit the article. It was published in 1995.

That same year, I mentioned another piece on the Anthro-L listserv. Rick Wilk recommended that I send it to business anthropologist John Sherry. It became a chapter titled "Malinowski, Magic and Advertising: On Choosing Metaphors" in Sherry's edited volume *Contemporary Marketing and Consumer Behavior: An Anthropological Source Book.* I eventually published a book titled *Japanese Consumer Behavior: From Worker Bees to Wary Shoppers.*

After being active for several years on Anthro-L, I discovered *Savage Minds* (now *Anthro {Dendrum}*) and the original Ning version of Keith Hart's *Open Anthropology Cooperative*. In some ways these sites were better than the schools where I had been a full-fledged academic. I could revel in the debate while blissfully free of the administrative busy work and publish-or-perish pressures that a "real academic career" entails.

COMING TO *POPANTH*

Erin

My own writing was going fairly well, but I wanted to read what others wrote and collectively discuss how we could improve our craft. There was, however, very little popular anthropology online.

In July 2012, I started the PopAnth group on the OAC and informed everyone that I was collecting links to popular anthropology articles. The first person to contribute a link was Keith Hart, who sent me an article he wrote for *openDemocracy*. Keith's comments were quickly followed by contributions from Liz Challinor, Daniel Lende, Gwendolen Lynch, and Huon Wardle. Liz commented, "It is an urgent task to devise ways of thinking and talking about the economy that make human sense." Daniel Lende suggested using humor to grab people's attention. Then, Gwendolen chimed in,

> The problem as Erin, myself and others have discussed extensively
> is that there [is] a vast amount of interesting and relative content
> that is produced by anthropologists that never sees the light of
> day outside of academia and that is not a good thing. Keith had

an interesting point in a Facebook discussion on this recently that there are too many people that you will never convince for a variety of reasons, however that still leaves a lot of people out there who are, as Erin describes it, "thinkers who are on the edge." So what would be awesome would be a pool of ideas that we can take to a broader audience to give them things to think about, and hopefully over time influence the wider discourse.

Liz immediately responded that we could count her in for our as-yet-undefined project. Greg Downey urged us to stop talking and start doing.

Gwendolen

Greg's comment was my call to action. Thirty minutes later, *PopAnth* was born. I registered the domain name, created accounts on social media, and sent the hyperlinks to people who had expressed interest in the project.

Our idea was not to just publish our own content but to search for and promote popular anthropology wherever it was published, raising the profile of the discipline and its authors.

How did we choose the name? As we brainstormed ideas, Daniel Lende started with popcorn analogies. I came up with *Hot Buttered Humanity*.

> *Our idea was not to just publish our own content but to search for and promote popular anthropology wherever it was published, raising the profile of the discipline and its authors.*

Then came the task of building the website. I wanted the website to promote not just its own articles, but also the authors who produce them and popular anthropology in general. It took a few months to design and build the features needed to achieve this broader goal.

I felt strongly – and still do – that in order for popular anthropology to be successful, the authors who write it need to become recognizable names. So I built in proper biographies for every author, links to their social media accounts, and pictorial bibliographies of their published books with relevant Amazon links to encourage sales. On the home page, I added a "PopStars" box with an author's picture and tag line. Every time a reader refreshes this page, a new PopStar pops up. This gives authors continued visibility on the website.

To promote popular anthropology generally, we did things like put visual links to TED talks by anthropologists on the home page. We added a visible link to our Twitter feed, which we used to share popular anthropology articles we found around the tracks. Additionally, I added a "Further Reading" section for each article, to encourage readers to engage with more material on the topic. As much as possible, we tried to suggest further reading that was open access and written for a general audience.

I also invested a substantial amount of time building discussion forums, both for readers to comment on articles and for the editorial process. How this worked was that an author would submit an article through the *PopAnth* portal and it would automatically go into our database, generating a discussion in the forum. The author and editors could then discuss the writing in the same place. This made the editorial process an open discussion rather than making editorial decisions behind closed doors. It also allowed the editors to work closely with the author to improve their piece.

John

In my case, being an anthropologist but making a living outside the ivory tower led to my searching for opportunities to contribute to academic debates. I also felt that I needed to pay back for a lucky and privileged life by offering a helping hand to younger anthropologists.

What could I offer? When I joined *PopAnth*, I became the "Writing Coach." I would not replace the editors who reviewed submissions and offered their own comments. I would offer suggestions for improving storytelling and narrative flow.

PURPOSE

Erin

We had several publics in mind. I thought about the reader. Anthropologists have lots of interesting stories that are very different from their academic analyses. I wanted people to be able to access these different, often quirky, stories. I especially had in mind people who were studying anthropology, had studied it before, or were generally interested in it. I wanted to provide something for these people. I was less interested in people who weren't interested in anthropology.

I saw my job at *PopAnth* as centered on making the writing readable. Most of my editorial work was less focused on the substance of the articles – I left that up to the likes of John and Laura. I asked myself, "Will this make sense to the reader?," focusing on things like whether the story flowed logically, whether there were specialist terms in need of explanation, enough paragraph breaks, and so on.

The whole experience was excellent training for me as a writer as well. In the first few months or so I picked up a lot from John about writing generally, including the great idea of deleting the first paragraph in a story in order to get over the waffle and straight to the point. John also pointed us toward excellent writing resources, which taught me about things like not using more words than necessary, using sentences of different length – lots of stuff. Then, the practice of editing for the public over the course of several years really hammered home my sense of storyline and readability. It has made me a much better writer.

John

I saw *PopAnth* as a space in which contributors could report discoveries that were not yet ready to be published in academic journals. For young anthropologists, it would be a space in which to introduce themselves. More senior anthropologists could contribute anecdotes of the type we share in bar conversations at professional meetings. At the same time, however, the contributions should be, ideally at least, anthropologically relevant, addressing issues in ways that connect observations in particular times and places to topics of theoretical interest.

Gwendolen

PopAnth's purpose was to change conversations. It was also to change the perception of what the discipline had to offer. I wanted conversations at dinner parties to be shaped by our output. I wanted industry to start demanding our expertise because of the change to the perception of our output's value. That goes back to the point about the increasing enrollments at universities and the need to find funding, as well as the need for anthropology graduates to find jobs.

Rather than anthropologists having to fight for recognition, I wanted to see the day where it was commonplace for the CEO of a major organization to turn to his or her trusted people and say, "Bring me the anthropologist!"

Rather than anthropologists having to fight for recognition, I wanted to see the day where it was commonplace for the CEO of a major organization to turn to his or her trusted people and say, "Bring me the anthropologist!"

WHAT WORKED. WHAT DIDN'T WORK.

Laura

PopAnth was very successful at doing what it set out to do. I was impressed at the efforts to make sure the articles were well written and interesting. The use of images and photographs was also successful.

I loved the articles that took everyday things and behaviors – especially those that are normalized, seemingly trivial, or taken for granted – and discussed them through the lens of anthropology. "An anthropologist's guide to choosing an engagement ring" and "The (il)logic of tipping: Why foreigners don't understand gratuities" were especially good, but the barriers to continuing success were high.

As an editorial board, we generated many great ideas, but we had trouble finding people willing to write essays. It's difficult to get anthropologists in academic positions to write essays that will not be considered worthy by review committees. Currently, I'm an associate editor for a forthcoming encyclopedia of linguistic anthropology, and we are running into this problem as well. It is a four-volume set with around 450 entries. The pool of potential writers is small, and they began to complain when asked to write essays for this and several other similar projects. *PopAnth* was also dependent on unpaid academics, graduate students, and professionals to contribute essays.

Lack of funding was a serious problem. The concept for *PopAnth* was fresh and exciting, and it caught the attention of people at the Wenner-Gren Foundation, who launched their own version of *PopAnth*, called *SAPIENS*, in 2016. Wenner-Gren was able to pay for professional journalists, anthropology contributors, and full-time paid staff editors, copy editors, and layout artists to support the site. With the prestige value of the Wenner-Gren, they were also able to syndicate articles with mainstream media outlets such as *Slate, The Atlantic,* and so on. *PopAnth* was a small operation that couldn't compete with that. Our team were unpaid writers and editors who had competing jobs and professional commitments.

Liz

I responded to the invitation to become an editor because I was involved in the *Open Anthropology Cooperative* and enjoyed exchanging ideas in an informal fashion. These discussions were particularly appealing because I worked a lot from home and chances to interact with colleagues were rare. I "met" Erin through OAC. She invited me to become a *PopAnth* editor.

To me, the main point of *PopAnth* was to make the anthropological way of seeing the world available to a wider audience. As I see it, anthropology has a lot to offer to the general public, but we anthropologists stay closed inside our academic circles. I see anthropology as questioning (culturally) received wisdom.

It is also interesting to write for a non-anthropological readership because you have to avoid academic jargon and can't "short cut" your thinking for colleagues who are "in the know" – you have to spell it all out, a very interesting exercise because it makes you look at and question what you (think you) know from different angles.

I also liked the idea of being able to write about an issue or topic on which you may not be a specialist but may still have something valuable to say. *PopAnth* provided an opportunity to use data or draw on experiences in a freer way.

I also appreciated the dialogue made possible by allowing readers to comment and to contribute to online discussions. It is very important for anthropology to contribute to current debates.

My overall experience with *PopAnth* was positive. As an editor, I learned about a range of topics. As a writer, I enjoyed writing the articles and seeing them published in a timely manner. This felt good when academic articles can take up to two years to be published. It also felt good to be able to write and read short pieces that were not full-length articles but covered interesting empirical and theoretical material.

Celia

I got involved with *PopAnth* first as a writer, pitching a piece or two that might be funny and engaging for readers. When I was invited to become an editor, I appreciated the chance to see how a collaborative website works "backstage," assessing submitted articles, recruiting writers, and providing feedback on works in progress. I wanted to help promote anthropology for a general audience, and *PopAnth* seemed like a good community in which to work experimentally toward that goal.

As a writer, I found the feedback I got from editors both critical and supportive; as an editor, I experienced collaboration and mutual support. I never fully vibed with the site design and colors, to be honest, but I absolutely loved what the site was doing. I appreciated the chance to get popularly oriented articles out beyond my own blog, to a community of readers who were interested in new takes on culture.

I also valued the chance to coach newer anthropologists on their writing and help them reshape academic ideas for a more popular audience. Sometimes the articles for which we provided coaching still felt like works in progress – but this progress offered authors the opportunity to develop beyond the conventions of academic speech and reach new readers.

As a reader, I find long-form reflections engaging. I see the value in the glossy and heavily edited and marketed anthropology articles at sites like *SAPIENS*, which are designed to be shared. I've produced popular anthropology articles for the web, but because they don't "count" for academic review, are unpaid, and haven't particularly drawn readership, it's hard to feel a sustained energy to continue producing something that produces only modest results for me and others.

In an age of surplus, I also find it hard to promote the best work that I'm reading. Few of my friends use RSS feeds, and many seem to rely on ad-revenue-driven algorithmic sites like Facebook and Twitter to select news for them. The popular anthropology articles I post to those sites aren't selected by the algorithm. I've wondered if I should post pictures of my hand with an engagement ring, or keys to a new house … something that will trigger the algorithms to promote the post widely … then slip a critique of romance or nuclear-family structures into the comments?

I've watched public intellectuals like Zeynep Tufekci set up private mailing lists in an attempt to provide a space for communication to followers outside the algorithms that jumble cute memes with ecological tragedy. But she's still within the same system; I find it hard to attend to her long-form email when I know there's an engaging web game around the corner. I try to inject popular anthropology into our experience of the internet ... and yet I find myself drawn in and transformed by these same social sites, posting for the rewards I get instead of saying what's really on my mind.

What does that mean for public anthropology? One possibility is more short videos, more fact lists, more memes that link to public anthropology websites, more integration with advertising. Another might be to sidestep these powerful forces: to offer in-person classes on how to take back your attention or coffee meetups in local real spaces. If we don't help folks to create space, where will we find the space for public anthropology?

REFLECTIONS

Gwendolen

PopAnth ended up being a catalyst for bringing some of these discussions front and center inside the discipline. We were able to host a town hall at an AAA meeting. We produced a booklet called "Showcasing Popular Anthropology" that aggregated popular anthropology from all kinds of sources, and, along with Natalia Reagan, we made a video about popular anthropology. We created connections among people who are very passionate about these topics in this space. That was really good, but for me it underlines the importance of engaging communities to help create and continue discussions and effect changes.

I see stuff like this as being instrumental, but the fact that it comes and goes is great; that in itself is a positive and leaves space for other people to step up and try something else. But people won't combine efforts. Everyone wants to change the world and have these conversations, but there are not enough people doing it. Ultimately this limits our ability to change the discipline's reputation. We're getting there, but slowly. Professional organizations like the Ethnographic Praxis in Industry Community (EPIC) tend to have more direct impact here.

Erin

I have long felt that if anthropology has a <u>unique sales proposition</u> (USP), it is our willingness to analyze anything through a cultural lens and, having taken a step back, to ask, "What do we do and why do we do it?"

I have long felt that if anthropology has a unique sales proposition, it is our willingness to analyze anything through a cultural lens and, having taken a step back, to ask, "What do we do and why do we do it?"

The first book I encountered that really opened my eyes to this approach was *American Kinship* (1968) by David Schneider. That book taught me that anything can be subject to analysis, to being broken down and built back up again.

PopAnth embraced this stance by carrying pieces on topics including toilet brushes, war, engagement rings, and Bic for Her pens. We wanted to make people rethink their assumptions about the world around them.

The conversations editors had with writers reflected this goal. On many occasions, feedback from John or Laura included the comment, "Interesting … but so what?" The "so what?" was critical to push authors to build up their piece from an interesting story into an anthropological insight.

SUCCESS

Erin

Tracking the stories submitted to *PopAnth* was fun. They covered a huge range of topics and many were very much off-the-wall. I loved it. It demonstrated to me that anthropologists have tons of material in their field notes and imaginations that never sees the light of day. It isn't suitable for books or journal articles, and there are even fewer blogs that will accept this kind of material. I was very proud that we could publish it.

I am personally happy with what we achieved. It was (and still is) an interesting experiment that pushed the boundaries of what short-form anthropology can be. When I visit the *PopAnth* website today, I am proud to see a really interesting collection of articles that I would happily sit down and read again. Few of them have gone out of date. Whether we continue to publish or not, *PopAnth* remains a great resource for anthropologists, students, and the general public to delve into.

The question I am left with is: Why is this kind of material rarely published? Certainly it isn't standard. Is it that readers aren't interested, or that they can't find it, or that writers don't think of publishing it?

John

I agree that anything related to humanity is grist for the anthropological mill. The ad-man in me asks, "Why should anyone not immersed in this particular hobby or obsessed with this particular cause care about this topic?" When anthropology repeats familiar clichés or addresses only problems of local interest, it loses the appeal I used to find in the study of humanity in all of its diversity.

The "reward" for writing, reading, or editing *PopAnth* is the central issue. Initial altruistic enthusiasm gives way to realization that work is required and, thus, to the question, "In exchange for what?" Acceptable rewards are narrowing to being paid or scoring points toward promotion or tenure. The idea that writing can be fun and writing to learn can be a way to contribute to a growing body of knowledge is disappearing.

Popular anthropology must now compete with other online material that also includes touching personal encounters, exotic bits of information, and political attitudes. The ad-man sees a lack of a compelling proposition to break through that clutter, attract authors and readers, and bring them back for more.

What that proposition might be is a difficult question. The answer may differ for authors, readers, and editors.

As an author, I seek recognition that may lead to other rewards. Returning to academic writing as a hobby has been richly rewarding, an opportunity to make new friends, learn new things, be invited to conferences, and return to teaching without the burdens of academic administration that my full-time academic friends endure. Would writing for *PopAnth* have produced these results? No.

As a reader, I look for something more than the touching personal encounters and clichéd political stances. I look for new angles on classic debates. I count as particularly rewarding pointers to work, sometimes whole new fields of knowledge, of which I have been oblivious.

I see potential in sites like *Geek Anthropologist* or the now notorious journal *HAU*. Both are built around clear intellectual commitments, to "All things Geek" and "Ethnographic Theory," respectively.

Which brings me back to the question: What is our USP? What is the proposition that would engage the interest and build a community dedicated to ongoing dialogue, dialogue that is "good to think with," as well as cute, funny, or critical? Increasingly, I see this as a question for anthropology as a whole, not just for *PopAnth* alone.

In *Agricultural Involution* (1963), Clifford Geertz describes a growing population of Javanese peasants cultivating smaller and smaller plots of land more and more intensively. The result was deepening poverty. When I look at social and cultural anthropology today, I see "ethnographic involution." Putting aside a few prominent exceptions (Descola, Kohn, and Tsing, for example) [anthropologists write about smaller and smaller, largely unrelated topics. The field as a whole becomes increasingly impoverished.]

These thoughts may be nothing more than impressions biased by what I read on- and offline. They do, however, seem to me to apply both to *PopAnth* and its predecessor, the *Open Anthropology Cooperative*. Both adopted a fully open, "let a thousand flowers bloom" strategy. The purpose was noble, the execution quixotic. In the title of one of his books, Japanese star copywriter Takashi Nakahata observes, "If you try to please everyone, everyone will hate you." "Hate" may be too strong. "Indifference" is more likely.

FOR DISCUSSION

1 *PopAnth* was an experiment to see which topics anthropologists would write about when they had the kind of creative freedom you don't get writing for journals. Which topics might you write about if you were not constrained by a particular research trajectory or journal convention?

2 The knowledge gathered by ethnographers can assist members of the general public in understanding

"differences" and the (cultural) reasoning behind them. Which public spaces, in particular, could benefit from these kinds of understandings?

3 Popular anthropology can help to counter the flawed assumption that humans are rational actors and tear down assumptions created by misinformation. Identify a common misconception about human behavior that has entered the popular consciousness and discuss how anthropology might address it.

4 What captures the interest of an anthropologist is not always what captures the interest of wide audiences. Think about an article you might write for the public. Answer the question: "What makes this worth knowing?"

ACKNOWLEDGMENTS

The authors would like to thank Laura Miller, Celia Emmelhainz, and Elizabeth Challinor for their input into this chapter.

REFERENCES

Geertz, C. 1963. *Agricultural Involution: The Process of Ecological Change in Indonesia*, Vol. 11. Berkeley: University of California Press.

Haviland, W.A., H.E. Prins, B. McBride, and D. Walrath. 2013. *Cultural Anthropology: The Human Challenge*. Boston: Cengage Learning.

McCreery, John Linwood. 1990. "Why Don't We See Some Real Money Here? Offerings in Chinese Religion." *Journal of Chinese Religions* 18, no. 1: 1–24.

McCreery, John. 1995a. "Malinowski, Magic and Advertising: On Choosing Metaphors." In *Contemporary Marketing and Consumer Behavior*, edited by John F. Sherry Jr., 309–29. Thousand Oaks: SAGE.

McCreery, John. 1995b. "Negotiating with Demons: The Uses of Magical Language." *American Ethnologist* 22, no. 1: 144–64.

McCreery, John Linwood. 2000. *Japanese Consumer Behavior: From Worker Bees to Wary Shoppers*. New York: Routledge.

Schneider, D.M. 2014. *American Kinship: A Cultural Account*. Chicago: University of Chicago Press.

CHAPTER SIX

SAPIENS: An Origins Story

Chip Colwell and Leslie Aiello

IMAGINING *SAPIENS*

The origins of the online magazine *SAPIENS* began in a hotel room, late one sleepless night. Chip was watching the food writer Anthony Bourdain sitting in a fast food stall, stuffing himself with a steaming mound of golden fried chicken and French fries. Across from him was a woman covered in an abaya, only her hands and cherubic face exposed amid the flowing black cloth. Their booth had high doors that swung closed, keeping the outside world from seeing the dining couple. With greasy fingers and full mouths, they casually chatted about how to eat fast food – Saudi Arabian style.

The moment was classic Bourdain, as presented on his TV show *No Reservations*, a program ostensibly about food but actually about culture. In this episode, Bourdain was the stranger lost in Arabia, the disoriented outsider struggling to make sense of a world vastly different from his own. There in the Middle East, his liberal politics, propensity for profanity and the profane, his love of strong alcohol, and all-night binges were as out of place as an orchid growing on the moon.

Bourdain opened his mind by eating his way through Saudi Arabia. He immersed himself in this foreign land by feasting on offal for breakfast, camel for lunch, a snack of sautéed lizard (a Bedouin delicacy), and fast food for dinner. But consuming these different foods was just an excuse for talking about difference. Bourdain seriously inquired about Islam. He observed conspicuous consumption at a mall. He charted a family's history. He questioned if national borders are evaporating in the face of globalization. By journey's end, Bourdain thoughtfully contrasted Saudi life with his own home in New York, concluding that he should not judge another culture by his own values.

By the show's end, Chip had this revelation: *No Reservations* was not a travel show or a food show. It was an anthropology show – only without any anthropologists. Chip realized that there was potentially a huge appetite for the work of anthropology – if only anthropologists could figure out how to make their work compelling and captivating to the outside world. He looked around and thought of how online magazines like *Slate* and *Huffington Post* capitalized on the internet's ability to produce articles quickly that could speak directly to international audiences. What if, he thought, there was a magazine like those, but authored by the discipline itself?

In 2014, Chip had an unexpected chance to pursue this idea. He was attending a symposium hosted by the Wenner-Gren Foundation for Anthropological Research in Sintra, Portugal. In a lush former-palace-turned-hotel, the workshop attendees were chatting after a long day. Somehow the conversation arrived at the question of public anthropology. Leslie, then the foundation's president, began to wonder aloud about what the next big project for the field might look like. What could the field really do to connect with a broad public? Chip asked Leslie if they could have breakfast the next morning. The beginnings of a plan were hatched.

We agreed that the public generally loved well-presented anthropological stories without realizing that what they loved was anthropology.

We agreed that the public generally loved well-presented anthropological stories without realizing that what they loved was anthropology.

The field was experiencing a public perception crisis and had also become the brunt of political jabs about the irrelevance of the social sciences and wastefulness of public spending. A substantial number of anthropologists, many of whom are included in this volume, were trying to buck this trend and engage the public. But the effort was often scattered, driven by the ability of motivated scholars as individuals to figure out how to publish an op-ed or start a blog or interest a journalist in a story or write in a clear and engaging manner. Even those most dedicated to reaching the public too often failed to meaningfully reach a broad audience.

The limits of efforts could be narrowed to three key problems, we felt.

1 There was no single, well-known outlet that aggregated and presented original anthropologically driven content for a public audience.

2 Numerous scholars were interested in inserting their work into the public sphere but too often lacked the training to effectively do so.

3 Presenting anthropology to the public still lacked prestige within the academy. 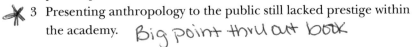 Big point thru out book

CREATING *SAPIENS*

What could Chip and Leslie and the Wenner-Gren Foundation do to help avert anthropology's potential spiral of irrelevance?

The will was there and the Wenner-Gren Foundation was also in the unique position to do something about it. Founded in 1941 with the specific aim of supporting academic research in anthropology, the foundation felt the "spiral of irrelevance" acutely. The timing of this need was also perfect. The foundation was laying plans for its seventy-fifth anniversary in 2016 and mulling over ways in which its relatively modest – but still significant – endowment could continue to provide meaningful support to the discipline for the next 75 years.

The potential of launching a large public outreach initiative was a novel (and frankly scary) idea for Wenner-Gren, which had no prior experience or expertise in public outreach or the media. For 75 years, its sole mission was to fund international research and networking in the academic discipline, leaving the public dissemination of research to others. But because of the crisis in the perception of anthropology, the idea turned out to be a relatively easy sell to the foundations' board of trustees, who were looking for an exciting project to take the foundation in a novel and relevant direction. The luxury of a private foundation (with no heirs of the founder to dictate how the money is spent) is that it can gamble on new and perhaps risky endeavors. And this is precisely what happened.

Once the go-ahead was given, reality struck. We had the resources behind us and now had to deliver, but at that stage, we had relatively little idea of how to do so. It was clear that simply providing a website for anthropologists to post what they felt were articles suitable for the public was naive. We were aiming to be the *Slate*, *Vox*, or *Huffington Post* of anthropology. We needed help.

And help is what we got. At first we stayed close to home in New York City and engaged a web consultancy company to help us think through seemingly simple things like what to call the magazine (the name *SAPIENS* did not come easily!), who our target audience was (we settled on international English-speaking adults with a curiosity about the world), and the nature of our online presence (we ultimately decided to provide more original content than an aggregator). We also reached out to other foundations with similar initiatives (e.g., the Simons Foundation, which funds the online science magazine *Quanta*), who provided welcome insight into what it takes to run a professional science communication initiative.

Two things quickly became clear. We needed a professional science communicator on board as a full-time employee to help shape the tone of the publication to reach our target audience. We also needed serious consultancy services to design and roll out the website and, after launch, to grow the readership.

Both of these were accomplished early in 2015, less than a year before our planned launch in January 2016, Wenner-Gren's anniversary year. After extensive searches, Amanda Mascarelli was hired as the managing editor and Abstract Edge as our web developer. At this stage, Chip and Leslie (and Amanda) still did not realize the work that was in front of us. The people at Abstract Edge probably did, though! Throughout the summer and fall of 2015, hours upon hours were spent on the web design – including everything from the minutiae of font choice and color palette to page layout and content categorization.

When the website was well enough along, our attention turned to rollout and content promotion. Chip and Amanda established editorial processes and began to seek out authors so that *SAPIENS* would launch with articles that would ensure it was immediately perceived as the serious, fascinating, and accessible anthropological publication that we all had set our sights on.

SAPIENS was launched on January 28, 2016, with the mission to "become a leading public voice for anthropology by publishing great stories that spark meaningful conversations around the world about anthropological ideas, theories, and discoveries." The content is focused on the development of a public voice for anthropologists by bringing together scholars and journalists to regularly publish relevant, expert, exciting, and accessible articles that explore all areas of the discipline. The intent is to build a vast international readership of laypeople interested in "everything human" and to spark meaningful conversations about anthropology's ideas, theories, and discoveries in the public sphere. The launch was successful beyond our expectations and we all felt that our hard work had paid off – but how was SAPIENS going to continue to realize this vision?

REALIZING SAPIENS

Here's how SAPIENS typically works: A potential author pitches an article idea to the editorial team. (The pitch is a brief summary and a short sample.) If the team thinks it's a good fit, we commission a full draft. That full draft is submitted and reviewed, and if workable, it goes into the editorial pipeline. The first few drafts are undertaken with a developmental editor. Once finalized, it is reviewed by the managing editor and editor-in-chief; a copy editor edits and fact checks it. The piece is then uploaded to the website, reviewed by at least three people, and published. The magazine's digital editor then promotes the piece online, mainly on social media. This is the core work of the magazine, aiming to publish two original pieces each week, almost every week of every year.

Throughout this process, contributing anthropologists learn about the processes popular magazines use (e.g., how to pitch). They also gain insights into the craft of writing, developing skills in storytelling, building tension, developing characters, and adding color – all while staying grounded in anthropological research. Once their piece has been published, authors learn about the digital media landscape and how anthropology is viewed by different publics. Many contributors have told us how widely their piece has been read. One told us that for the first time, his mother understood his research. Another told us that her university dean took note of her work for the first time. A regular columnist has reoriented his entire career toward popular writing, once he compared the hundreds of readers he has for his academic articles to the hundreds of thousands of readers he receives for his popular articles.

Maintaining the magazine also involves managing the employees (a mix of seven full and part time, who are all absolutely essential to the magazine's success), keeping the website running smoothly, budgeting, designing and implementing marketing plans, holding workshops on writing, publishing a weekly email newsletter, and many more details big and small.

In short, it's a lot of work!

There are many ways to measure and quantify the magazine's progress. We regularly review a range of analytics. Here are a few that stand out in the magazine's first five years:

- We published nearly 500 articles.
- Our articles were read nearly 15 million times on sapiens.org.
- Dozens of articles were republished, including online through *The Atlantic*, *Scientific American*, and *Discover Magazine*.
- We amassed more than 72,000 Facebook followers, 21,000 Twitter followers, and 30,000 email subscribers.
- "The Darkest Truths," by Elizabeth Svoboda, won the 2017 Society for American Archaeology's Gene Stuart Award.
- "Natural Disasters Are Social Disasters," by Dana Graef, was listed as a notable essay in *The Best American Science and Nature Writing 2018*.
- We won the 2017 American Anthropological Association General Anthropology Division's New Directions Group Award.
- We won the 2018 American Anthropological Association's Executive Director's Award.
- "Unearthing the True Toll of the Tulsa Race Massacre," by Megan I. Gannon, won the 2020 Society for American Archaeology's Gene Stuart Award.

In 2018, the Wenner-Gren Foundation invested in the addition of *SAPIENS: A Podcast for Everything Human*. The podcast was on Apple's New and Noteworthy list for three weeks running. The episodes from the first season have now been downloaded more than 200,000 times across 154 countries – putting the show in the top five science podcasts on Apple and in the top 400 podcasts on all of Apple (out of 550,000) during its run.

Planning for future seasons is underway. The next year, additional areas for growth included a new postdoctoral fellowship position on the team and workshops to provide more training for anthropologists and students.

While our readership has steadily grown each year – from under one million readers in 2016 to more than four million in 2020 – our very first challenge was to attract any readers at all. As a brand new media endeavor, we didn't have any readers.

Although our target audience is non-anthropologists, we figured the best place to start was with the anthropological community.

Although our target audience is non-anthropologists, we figured the best place to start was with the anthropological community.

We started letting our colleagues know about the magazine through our networks, then promoting the pending launch at the 2015 annual meeting of the American Anthropological Association. We also had the advantage of Wenner-Gren's network and sent out email blasts to former grantees. By the time the magazine launched, we had an initial email list of about 2,000 people.

A fundamental challenge to this project has been finding strategies that allow *SAPIENS'* articles to find traction in today's overcrowded media landscape. We have learned that few readers simply come to sapiens.org to see what's new (only about 4 percent of our readers even go to the magazine's home page). Instead, we must "sell" each and every article on its own. Most readers come to an article from a social media channel, read the article, and then leave to go to a different article from a different source.

This reality requires us to invest time in developing a marketing approach that will bring readers to each article on its own. For example, the editorial team spends an enormous amount of energy developing titles that will pull readers in without coming too close to clickbait. The magazine's digital editor does yeoman's work on social media to circulate each article and try to create new and meaningful conversations (not so easy in today's manic digital environment).

Despite all the effort, one frustration is that there is no clear winning formula. Some articles seem to have all the right elements – exceptionally well written, clever title, timed with current conversations – and yet may not do well. In turn, other pieces might not seem to have all parts perfected but then attract lots of readers or engage lots of people in great conversations. This is a common theme for our peer magazines as well. Not long ago, an editor from a major online magazine asked colleagues to help explain why an article about treating teenage drug abuse in Iceland went viral. We're not sure anyone had a good answer.

The key to this work has been the relationships the magazine has formed with various partners, from our colleagues at magazines like *The Atlantic*, who republish pieces, to academic journal editors, who help bring new writers in, to the American Anthropological Association, which helps promote articles and the podcast, to *SAPIENS'* advisory board of anthropologists. Central to the endeavor has also been the relationships between the Wenner-Gren Foundation's board and advisors, its staff, who do much of the behind-the-scenes work, and the magazine's own staff. These three nodes create a nexus that sustains the magazine's daily work and enables it to learn and grow.

While professional relationships have been important, unquestionably the most important element that has made this project possible is its relationship to the Wenner-Gren Foundation. When Chip envisioned this project, he hoped for the support of the foundation not only because of its ability to fund the magazine but also to build on its status and goodwill within the discipline. What he didn't realize at the start was that the foundation also held a diverse board with expertise in many areas relevant to the magazine – such as law, open access, science communication – and that the foundation's staff would embrace the new project so wholeheartedly.

In the end, though, what the magazine depends on most is the respect and support of the anthropological community itself. While the magazine needs an audience, without the buy-in of anthropologists there wouldn't be any stories – no content – for the public to read. For this, we're so grateful that so many anthropologists have written for the magazine, contributing their insights and labor to the larger vision of making anthropology relevant and engaging for a broad public.

CONTINUING *SAPIENS*

We acknowledge that it is anthropologists themselves who have helped make the magazine better. Particularly at the beginning of the endeavor, the magazine didn't have smooth and clear processes for writers. Gradually, we improved (or hope we did) by streamlining the editorial process and making that process clearer to authors at the start of each piece.

This editorial process is truly at the heart of the magazine. We decided early on that we'd either live or die by the quality of *SAPIENS'* content. Already by 2015, the internet was a crowded place with no shortage of articles and opinions. The way we would stand out and try to carve out a clearer space for anthropology would be by developing a magazine with stories that could just as easily have been published in *National Geographic* or the *New York Times Magazine.*

This high standard, we think, has been a hallmark of *SAPIENS* but also one of its greatest challenges yet. First, this is a challenge in that the world's greatest science magazines invest huge amounts of time and money into the editing process. For the foundation, which funds the magazine, there is a clear commitment to high standards, but this must be tempered by the reality of exhaustible budgets. Second, this is challenging because so few anthropologists are trained to write for a public audience. Hence, rather than working with journalists, who have spent years learning to write for non-scholars, *SAPIENS'* anthropologists are often "learning while doing" – developing the craft of writing for the public as they're doing it.

Although this challenge and many others present themselves daily to us, we do feel that the project's vision is being realized. We hope that this project helps many anthropologists find their voice in the wilderness of the internet and that it demonstrates the value of public engagement for anthropology. For future public anthropology projects, we recommend that they have a clear vision, find key partners, search out and secure sustainable funding, and seek the buy-in of anthropologists first and their target audience second. If the discipline can learn to do all this, then the next Anthony Bourdain-like series will actually be hosted by an anthropologist.

FOR DISCUSSION

1 Anthropology is a discipline that is compelling and cool to most members of the public, but anthropologists are rarely household names. Why do you think there are no anthropologists as famous as Anthony Bourdain?

2 *SAPIENS* provides a platform and training experience for anthropologists to write for the public. What would it take for the discipline to provide more outlets like *SAPIENS*? What do these outlets look like?

3 Anthropology has a long history of disciplinary divides and competing objectives around its role in conversations about what it means to be human. How can anthropology balance its goals of academic discourse and public engagement? *Should* anthropology make such a balance, or should it lean one way or the other? Why?

4 Anthropologists, as a whole, would like their work to be widely read. What do you see as barriers to more anthropologists writing for venues such as *SAPIENS*? How can these barriers be dismantled?

REFERENCES

Gannon, Megan I. 2020. "Unearthing the True Toll of the Tulsa Race Massacre." *SAPIENS*, May 22. https://www.sapiens.org/news/tulsa-race-massacre/.

Graef, Dana. 2017. "Natural Disasters Are Social Disasters." *SAPIENS*, December 13. https://www.sapiens.org/column/the-climate-report/hurricane-harvey-inequality/.

Svoboda, Elizabeth. 2016. "The Darkest Truths." *SAPIENS*, February 4. https://www.sapiens.org/archaeology/the-darkest-truths/.

PART THREE

Reimaging Public Spaces

CHAPTER SEVEN

Visualizing Immigrant Phoenix: An Urban Visual Ethnographic Collaborative

Kristin Koptiuch

Flying below the radar of official planning instruments and public acknowledgment, migrants are busily transforming metropolitan Phoenix. Visualizing Immigrant Phoenix, a student-faculty ethnographic research collaborative at Arizona State University–West, engaged undergraduate researchers in meaningful qualitative fieldwork in their local community to explore migrant displacements and urban transformations through visual documentation of immigrants' everyday imprint upon the Phoenix cityscape. The project results materialized as a lively website, several interactive exhibitions, and a digital mini-video production.

In the context of anti-immigrant Arizona, our vibrant photographic ethnographics accompanying the researchers' short, evocative field-based accounts offer viewers a visually rich (en)counter-narrative that embraces the transformative, creative, and potentially subversive power of migrant everyday mobilities in the city.

Our vibrant photographic ethnographics accompanying the researchers' short, evocative field-based accounts offer viewers a visually rich (en)counter-narrative that embraces the transformative, creative, and potentially subversive power of migrant everyday mobilities in the city.

This chapter presents my account of the impetus, context, and enactment of what turned out to be a very cool anthropology adventure in beyond-the-classroom learning.

GETTING STARTED AND DEVELOPING THE PROJECT

Visualizing Immigrant Phoenix is an extension of my long-term commitment to teaching, researching, and visualizing the impact of immigrants on metropolitan Phoenix, where I lived for nearly 27 years. Having long taught courses to Arizona youth on migration, diversity, and urbanism, and having worked with local migrant and refugee advocacy organizations and activists, I understood that Arizonans' hypersensitivity toward immigration could not easily be dissuaded by factual argumentation. Simply supplying accurate information did not upend deep-seated assumptions about the purported deleterious impact of immigrants in our midst. I devised pedagogical strategies to address emotion and affect as much as empirical fact, and I began to create ethnographic photo essays grounded in my own local field observations of migrants in an effort to use visualization to turn preconceived judgment into critical enjoyment.

A photo essay I contributed to Urban Vignettes, "Cruzando Fronteras/Crossing Phoenix," initiated this trajectory in visual ethnography (Koptiuch 2012). The piece interprets a huge billboard ad that used a border-crossing trope to publicize a popular California Latinx radio program. After its sudden appearance on a busy corner in my neighborhood, the billboard vanished almost immediately. I suggested that it had metaphorically hit a nerve by visualizing the nearly ineffable truth that no national wall could deter: "The border" had already crossed Phoenix. The positive reception of this essay by my students affirmed my suspicion that visual ethnography could make a subtle but effective tactic to crack open the persistent Arizona default perspective that perceives migrants solely as problem figures. I decided to integrate undergraduates into this initiative. My courses on migration and culture, social anthropology, and urban studies became research training labs for future ethnographers in what would become Visualizing Immigrant Phoenix.

The project took off after I successfully applied for modest funding intended to encourage student-faculty research. ASU's New College Undergraduate Inquiry and Research Experiences (NCUIRE) funds teams of four to six undergraduates who receive $625 (or two "free" credit hours) to work with faculty on a semester-long guided research project. Each team also receives a "supplies" budget of $500. NCUIRE's award activities occur on top of a student's course work, the incentive being the experience, honor, and recognition as a recipient of the re-sume-building award. Running my first team of five undergrads in Fall 2016 thoroughly surpassed my expectations in terms of the insight, ex-citement, and dedication that the student researchers brought to the project. The power of our collaborative effort surpassed the capabilities of the prototypical lone-gunslinger anthropologist.

I ran two more NCUIRE-funded research teams of five or six students in Spring 2017 and 2018, and together we created Visualizing Immi-grant Phoenix. I recruited team members both by individual invitation and by soliciting volunteers in my classes. This became an easy sell once we'd started the project and students could see how cool it was by re-viewing the website or testimony from previous team members. I facili-tated continuity by carrying over one or two students to the next team as research assistants, another category of NCUIRE funding. The re-searchers majored in a variety of fields (my School of Social & Behavio-ral Sciences offered only a minor in sociocultural anthropology), but all had taken at least one course with me, learning about critical concepts in ethnographic fieldwork, transnational migration, and urban studies. Additional brief training in digital documentation and ethnography on an initial joint field visit galvanized the teams' readiness to document migrants' everyday activities, businesses, artifacts, and neighborhoods. Each researcher's visual and ethnographic research skills and insights varied according to their major, ethnicity, generational linkage to mi-grant origins, multiple-language proficiency, and personal experiences in Phoenix communities. Inclusion of first-generation Assyrian Iraqi, Mexican, and Somali team members extended the project's reach and depth of insight into diverse migrant communities. The resultant in-terdisciplinary, interethnic synergies worked to the project's advantage, enriched by students' different perspectives, understandings, and crea-tivity. Each researcher brought their unique gaze for depicting the city, enlarging the scope, richness, and diversity of the project.

Visualizing Immigrant Phoenix emerged and evolved organically out of their fieldwork. Individually or in pairs, the researchers con-ducted their own field observations and interviews. They decided on

Figure 7.1. Mural on exterior walls of Taqueria El Guerreerense, East McDowell Road, Phoenix, 2018.

topics by acting on leads from their own contacts with migrants, by brainstorming together about project ideas, or by diving off the deep end into a potentially interesting project. Our researchers at first found it awkward to introduce themselves to interviewees, shop owners, residents; we produced a project business card to explain and authenticate the researcher's identity and role. Showing interviewees our website on their mobiles made the project comprehensible. The students' excitement about their own intrepid fieldwork endeavors was infectious and influenced subsequent teams. Researchers submitted drafts of their ethnographic essays and photos, revised them in response to my editorial suggestions, and turned them into finished projects. At times, students were chagrined when I asked them to revise their text "again" or to "do a bit more background research" to help with their readers' understanding. But they were clearly thrilled once their finished stories appeared on our website, enlivened by marvelous photos and even audio and video. All their work is showcased on our open-access website, which uses the Jimdo web platform. I designed, created, and still

Figure 7.2. Migrant rights march, Phoenix, April 4, 2006. An astonishing 200,000 people marched through downtown Phoenix.

maintain the space as curator of this ethnographic collection of some 40 photo essays, interviews, and curated photo sets, documenting the presence and imprint of migrants upon the Phoenix cityscape.

RESPONDING TO CONTEXT: ANTI-IMMIGRANT PUBLICS AND ARIZONA MOBILITIES

Our project's timing was critical, as 2016–2018 was a time of seemingly purposeful instability in US national immigration policy and enforcement. Validated by the highest levels of state and national government, migrants had been increasingly demonized, criminalized, denied due process, displaced from legal status, from citizenship, from human rights. The situation for metro Phoenix's abundant immigrant populations was even worse than when the *New York Times* aptly dubbed

Figure 7.3. Wall mural in Marvale, Phoenix. By Christen Garden, 2016.

Arizona the "national capital of anti-immigrant laws and oppressive policing" (July 28, 2012) in the aftermath of the controversy ignited by the Arizona legislature's notorious "show me your papers" law, Senate Bill 1070, in 2010. Our project responded to this context by employing cool anthropology to accord due importance to migrants' creative impact on everyday urbanism in our transnationalizing city.

Stymied by reigning anti-immigrant sentiment, city residents and civic leaders had been reluctant to acknowledge – let alone to cultivate – creative and constructive ways that migrants already infused the city with their presence. Latinx scholars in urban planning have produced a burgeoning literature on "Latino placemaking" or "barrio urbanism" in an effort to "learn from" and integrate into planning the insights, inspirations, and ingenuity found in urban Latinx communities in Chicago, Dallas, Los Angeles, Philadelphia, and Phoenix (see, for example, Diaz 2005; Diaz and Torres 2012; Gonzalez 2017; Lara 2018; Rios and Vasques 2012; Sandoval 2009; Sandoval-Strausz 2019). But planners generally have not been responsive to or inclusive of Latinx residents. Metro Phoenix scarcely integrates migrants and their much-vaunted

Figure 7.4. Mekong Plaza, Mesa, AZ. By Cynthia Canez, 2016.

entrepreneurial proclivity into city planning design, for instance, yet anyone with open eyes can see migrants' imprint tangibly exhibited across the cityscape in residential neighborhoods and commercial shopping strips.

Our project discovered that it is not so much migrants themselves (a small percentage of whom may not be officially authorized) but their contribution to quotidian city life that goes undocumented, un-recognized, undervalued. Visualizing Immigrant Phoenix thus aimed to document, visualize, and enhance appreciation for already-present migrant self-representational activities.

MULTIPLE MODALITIES, MULTIPLE AUDIENCES

Migrants' city planning initiatives may be more unwitting than delib-erate. But as informal, unintentional urban planners-from-below, mi-grants adapt design features characteristic of their homelands to etch unmistakable global aesthetics, identities, and expectations into American urban landscapes. Such change is not welcomed by everyone. Visualizing Immigrant Phoenix sought to acknowledge this by opening itself up to broader audiences and adopting new modalities to do so.

We soon realized that no matter how amazingly cool and lively a website can be, it remains a collection walled in by a screen. It is also difficult to direct viewers to the site in order to make a meaningful intervention toward transforming a predominant urban imaginary dismissive of migrant contributions.

We sought a more interactive presentation modality to share with "live" audiences our visually stimulating and thought-provoking work, a modality that both preserved the visually rich digital format of the website presentations of migrant stories and also highlighted the immersive excitement and sense of discovery that the researchers experienced in their fieldwork encounters.

We sought a modality that both preserved the visually rich digital format of the website presentations of migrant stories and also highlighted the immersive excitement and sense of discovery that the researchers experienced in their fieldwork encounters.

We took a risk and decided to experiment with an exhibition. None of us, least of all me, had ever been involved in producing an exhibition to share our work. Nor did the Society for Applied Anthropology know quite what to do with our proposal to mount our first exhibit at their 2017 Albuquerque conference. Finally, they accepted my suggestion to allow us to set up the exhibit in the book fair space, where it could safely remain for two days of interactive display. Three students joined me at the conference to set up and staff the exhibit. It was a success! Audience members (particularly professors) expressed to me their astonishment that undergrads had conducted all the research, created such fabulous projects, and so cogently explained their work. This inspired us to do more exhibits.

We loosely organized our exhibition around the project's several themes of migrant everydayness (immigrant portraits, artifacts, events, neighborhoods, businesses, landscapes). It was anchored by a display of project photos enlarged to poster size and accompanied by brief, evocative text summaries. Short mini-movies animated the exhibit space as they played in an endless loop on (borrowed) video display screens. Sonic atmospherics came from a boombox playing audio captured at our field sites, grouped on a looped soundtrack. Website projection invited audience perusal on a laptop, although this was less successful in the busy exhibit space than enlarged printouts from the website placed in a couple of oversized portfolio books, which made the stories more readily available for viewers to quickly flip through. We created our own logo to "brand" the project and provided simple, colorfully designed takeaways to the audience in the form of business cards, bookmarks, and scannable QR codes that linked the audience's ubiquitous mobile phones to our website.

Key to the exhibit experience, however, was the presence of the undergraduate researchers themselves. The students engaged the audience by explaining their own and each other's projects, using the photos as prompts to make the scenes and stories come to life. Our audience became enraptured by the researchers' field experiences, and even our shyest team members blossomed with enthusiasm as they recounted their field research. An immersive exhibition layout invited viewers to walk through and around the photos to "interact" with the images and to pose questions that activated researcher storytelling.

To more fully engage the audience to the point where they had a stake in the exhibition by becoming part of it themselves, we devised a participatory "portrait booth" where viewers could frame themselves as migrants or migrant descendants from specific countries or affirm their solidarity as migrant allies (Figure 7.5). Dozens of audience members (including well-known anthropologists and other scholars) star in their own portraits on our website.

Our amateur exhibition grew organically as our collection of digital projects expanded with the work of each new research team. We used each team's shoestring supplies budget to create and curate additional exhibition materials. With each exhibit, we made adjustments, introduced new features, and adapted to different spaces as needed. Thanks to the interactivity of the exhibition, the overall experience was as fulfilling and exciting for us presenters as for the audience.

We mounted four full-scale in-person interactive exhibitions at national and local venues, and we won the top award at our campus annual research symposium. Our outputs also included a couple of scaled-down, pop-up exhibits, an invited photo essay based on our stories related to migrant youth for the blog *Youth Circulations* (Koptiuch 2017), and academic presentations. The five mini-videos we created for the 2018 Society

Figure 7.5. Photos taken of exhibit audience members at Visualizing Immigrant Phoenix's participatory portrait booth, Society for Applied Anthropology meetings, Albuquerque, NM, March 2017.

for Cultural Anthropology/Society for Visual Anthropology virtual conference became yet another modality to reach new audiences.

Just as the project brought minoritized city spaces into the academy for its consideration, so too did the project bring the academy into the community.

We wish we could have done more community exhibits. My own career got in the way of our plans to bring the exhibit to migrant community events and to public policymakers when I decided to retire from academia and moved out of state. Clearly, more could be done to take such a rich and inspiring exhibition beyond actual and proverbial walls.

Just as the project brought minoritized city spaces into the academy for its consideration, so too did the project bring the academy into the community.

ORDINARINESS AND THE CHALLENGES OF VISUAL DOCUMENTATION

Beyond the colorful images, delightful stories, and participatory portraits depicting everyday migrant crossings and contributions, Visualizing Immigrant Phoenix took seriously its critical charge as "cool
anthropology" to intervene in public perceptions of migrants in Phoenix. Our collaborative photographic ethnographics document migrants
engaged in everyday urbanism, and this ordinariness, it seems to me,
cuts through the impasse that blocks the receptivity of many Phoeni-
cians to comprehending migrant contributions to their city. Our stories
of migrants depict them as resilient, resourceful, and at times heroic,
innovative agents, but also as vulnerable to the often-malignant conse-
quences of being seen or not seen, being (mis)recognized or omitted
from recognition altogether. But above all, our stories depict migrants'
presence in the city, their already-there-ness, without taking up positions of didactic judgment on the nation's great immigration debate. If
documenting the everydayness of migrant contributions is tantamount
to sedition in the eyes of Arizona's anti-immigrant enthusiasts, then
perhaps herein lies the greatest subversive potential of our project. Two
examples support this contention.

First, a major challenge we confronted was that our exhibition should
avoid reducing the fluidity of migrant life to mere "pictures" for viewers'
consumption and, perhaps, romanticization. Although we invited the
subjects of our stories to attend our exhibitions, as far as I know this
occurred only once – but its effect on addressing our challenge was deci-
sive. A DACA (Deferred Action for Childhood Arrivals) recipient interviewed by team member Argenis Hurtado Moreno came to our exhibit
at Glendale Community College. As she stood next to a poster of her
portrait, flanked on its other side by her interviewer, the two of them
dialogued about the interview with small groups of audience members.
In essence, the portrait "came to life," averting the estrangement of
the image from lived experience. The result was a sort of performative
transformation "from work to text" (Barthes 1971). The exhibit display
suddenly became a demonstration, a discursive exchange in which viewers became interlocutors and experienced, in a sense, the (inter)activity
that had produced the photo-as-text. Any presumptive ideas set in place
by the viewers' effective angle of arrival (Ahmed 2010) that predisposed

Figure 7.6. Dialogue between author Argenis Hurtado Moreno and interviewee Griselda brought to life her exhibition portrait. Glendale, AZ, 2017.

them to fix a DACA recipient into the hierarchical category of "illegal" Other were burst asunder by the subversive, distance-obliterating force of dialogical exchange. That the DACA recipient interviewee is an alumnus of another community college nearby, speaks unaccented colloquial American English, and displays American youth mannerisms, dress, and self-presentation shifted her positionality from Other to one-of-us, confounding any mistaken identity of her as "alien." The author of the piece, too, disclosed to the audience his own status as a DACA recipient and GCC alum, doubly making strange any reduction of this complex, pluralized performative text to unanimated, distanced "work" estranged from an ongoing constitutive, dialogic movement. Like the border-crosser subjects of the now-performative text, this movement cut across the image-as-signifier, whose symbolic meaning could have come to a halt, and transformed it into a passage through the impasse of liminality faced by foreign-born but American-made youth who are *ni de aqui, ni de alla* (neither from here nor there).

Figure 7.7. Fuchsia house in South Phoenix, 2013.

Decisively, the work, the' photo composite, could no longer be mistaken as solely an object of consumption. The performative doubling of portrait and persona set in play a new collaborative reading that then encompassed the viewers, implicating them in a polysemic narrative – a social text – that left no space for an outside, distanced observer, a glib classification, a judgment. The pleasure of audience engagement in this complex and provocative performative text was palpable.

The second example of the subversive effect of documenting migrant everydayness starts from a question we cannot yet answer: Does the cool artful activism and clear relevancy of Visualizing Immigrant Phoenix equip our audience with enough DIY ethnographic insights to launch themselves into the social-text surround of the city itself, where they can engage their own autonomous appreciation for the creative culinary/cultural/civic challenges posed by its de facto diasporic remaking by migrants?

For many exhibit viewers, migrant remakings of the city engage systems of signification that at first glance seem alien to the familiar, highly standardized American design of mass-produced consumer urbanism. The latter uses codes that register order, compliance, blandness, conformity, homogeneity (think fast food chains, corporate gas stations and drug stores, national department stores and supermarkets, mass-produced housing subdivisions). In some city quarters, any disorder, boldness, color, hybridity, or other defiance of a standardized white middle class aesthetic is perceived as a threat, to be squelched by zoning regulations or homeowner association codes, covenants, and restrictions.

But in other quarters, the urban art/ifacts we documented operate beyond the auspices of planners and regulatory codes. Migrant businesses often colonize and flourish in the dead spaces made moribund by urban sprawl's centrifugal pull. Migrants rework the city with an exuberant color palette or distinctive architectural features that are beacons to their transnational communities. Their marketing pitch often integrates without tension the hybridity of the realistic and the fabulous. Exotic, traditional Mexican cultural elements, say, in the magical-realist redesign of a day-glow orange drive-thru taqueria that now inhabits the uncannily familiar architectural structure of an erstwhile iconic fast food paragon, firmly re-roots the migrant not in a nostalgic Mexico but in a blended, transnationalized space located well beyond

Figure 7.8. A child is enraptured by dancers performing *ballet folklórico* in the ersatz Mexican town plaza in Mercado de los Cielos, Desert Sky Mall, Maryvale, Phoenix, 2017.

the national border. At the same time, these elements disconcertingly re-route everyday urbanism by integrating the Mexican marvelous and metaphorical into the rationality and materiality of the American City (see Valdez Moses 2001; also Koptiuch 2019). Or the formerly conventional Desert Sky Mall, which lost its clientele due to white flight into the farther-flung privatopias of suburban sprawl, gets converted into Mercado de los Cielos, a bustling flea-market-like commercial anchor space catering to the Latinx and immigrant neighborhoods that now surround its location in Maryvale (Maryvale was Phoenix's Levitown, its first master planned suburb of mass-produced housing sold exclusively to working-class whites in the mid-1950s, prior to the civil rights era's anti-discrimination legislation). The Mercado is complete with

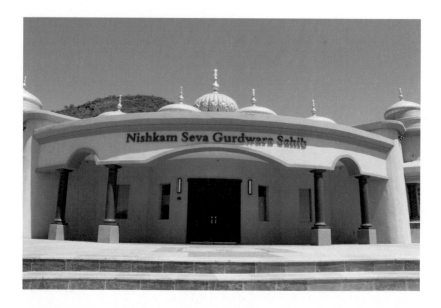

Figure 7.9. Nishkam Siva Gurdwara Sahib, Sikh place of worship, Glendale, AZ, by Nina Rocket, 2018 (*top*); Viet Nam Temple, west Phoenix, by Chrystin Sanchez, 2016 (*opposite page, top*); Wat Promkunaram, Thai Buddhist Temple of Arizona, Waddell, AZ, 2012 (*bottom*); Islamic Center of North Phoenix, Bosnian mosque, by Patrick Ingham, 2016 (*opposite page, bottom*).

Figure 7.10. Colorful mural on a can recycling center, East McDowell Road, Phoenix, February 2018. Researchers were shocked and saddened to discover that the colorful murals at the former can recycling center had been painted over so soon, East McDowell Road, Phoenix. By Nina Rocket, April 2018 (*opposite page*).

a lobby remake into an ersatz "town plaza" hosting traditional ballet folklórico to appreciative audiences of Latinx families sitting on "park benches" around the plaza, the children mesmerized by the costumed dancers. At local outposts of global religions, architectural flourishes on temples, mosques, and churches proudly signal that these spaces of worship are linked to elsewheres, their imported design as determined otherwise as has become the city itself (Figure 7.9).

All this creative urban reworking is accomplished by unconsecrated artists and craftspeople who transnationalize the city by using as their canvas the walls of neighborhood retail businesses like bakeries, restaurants, clothing shops, *llanteras* (tire shops), taquerias, *carnicerias* (meats and groceries), *yerberias* (medicinal herb shops).

Many of our stories highlight the exuberant visibility of immigrant urban remakings encountered by our researchers during fieldwork.

Taken together, they begin to map out an assemblage of collections of an exhibition in situ, already existing around Phoenix. Our hope is that our exhibition's intervention beyond the classroom and museum inspires our viewers and readers to venture beyond our project altogether, to cultivate their own appreciation for the extraordinary contributions made by migrants to the collective art of citymaking.

Our hope is that our exhibition's intervention beyond the classroom and museum inspires our viewers and readers to venture beyond our project altogether, to cultivate their own appreciation for the extraordinary contributions made by migrants to the collective art of citymaking.

Caution is warranted, in this respect. Our project also documents the vulnerability and ephemerality of some of these creative migrant collections, when their distinctive presence is not appreciated. Intrepid migrant entrepreneurs who brave the frontiers of disinvested neighborhoods find themselves at risk of displacement, sometimes due to their successful transformation of derelict urban spaces into the object of newly desirable reinvestment or gentrification. Some of our photo documentation of fabulous wall murals is now the only extant record of their existence, reminiscent of orphaned family photos found alongside the remains of migrants who perished so unnecessarily during their crossing, casualties of the callous "prevention through deterrence" model of immigration control that uses Arizona's Sonoran Desert as a killing machine (De León 2015). Painted-over murals or too-soon closed businesses made the affective pain of loss palpable among my research team; they'd come to appreciate sites they'd visualized and proprietors of shops they'd told stories about, only to find some had already been painted over, disappeared (Figure 7.10).

VISIONS REALIZED, LESSONS LEARNED

What we collaboratively accomplished in Visualizing Immigrant Phoenix exceeded my own personal expectations and expanded the far more modest vision with which we began the project. But I'd learned from having previously directed students in several other course-based ethnographic projects never to underestimate the capabilities and creativity of undergraduates. My only regret is that we did not have more time to push the project even further, before my retirement prematurely cut it off. Nonetheless, our collaborative research adventure accomplished a great deal, and the website still stands as a powerful record of this.

Visualizing Immigrant Phoenix did not so much aim to render visibility to migrants as to document their already visible but often unappreciated presence in our urban communities. We listened to migrant voices and stories already heard and told by migrants themselves and documented aspects of their everyday lives. We depicted their already-existing presence, making moot the question of whether they "belong." Migrant self-representation asserts itself in many ways, not always as intentional, agential activism for migrant rights and recognition and certainly not, as so frequently portrayed in media and public policy, primarily as agents of aggression or as disposable, non-contributing, worthless beings undeserving of basic human rights. Our project sleuthed out other ways, sometimes quiet and subtle, sometimes outlandishly exuberant, by which migrants embedded themselves in urban

Figure 7.11. *Dulcería* (candy store) run by Oaxacan migrants on East McDowell Road, Phoenix.

Phoenix. We learned firsthand that whereas migrant businesses and services are open to all, many also explicitly cater to a translocal community and bring to the city an insistent hybridity articulated through multiple languages, cultures, religions, subjectivities. By modifying and enlivening the city's urban design, migrants make it livable on their own terms.

By centering on migrants' everyday mobilities, our critical visualization strived to expand the appreciative embrace of immigrants in our city's collective imaginary. The city too is "on the move," transmogrifying right before our eyes from an ostensibly "American" city rooted in a fixed conception of nation, citizenship, and belonging into a mobile, border-defying, transnationalized site of local/global intersections linking economies, communities, cultural imaginaries. By exhibiting migrant everydayness in anti-immigrant Arizona, the interventions of Visualizing Immigrant Phoenix open fresh perspectives for envisioning alternative collective urban futures. Instead of proposing walls and fearful projections to exclude migrants, our stories and visualizations document definitively that they are already here, cogently representing themselves, living unthreatening, even salutary everyday lives alongside other Americans. Through these efforts, we tried to cut through the affective impasse that blocks the receptivity of many Arizonans to comprehend migrants' contributions so that they can embrace the transformative, potentially subversive power of the city's de facto diasporic remaking by migrants. Take a look at our website to see what you think!

FOR DISCUSSION

1 The Visualizing Immigrant Phoenix (VIP) team sought to engage public audiences in their project. What are other venues in which an interactive exhibition like VIP could make new connections with audiences outside academia?

2 By targeting affect as much as fact, VIP aims at the heart as much as the intellect. This approach to migrants' impact in/on the city required a combination of scholarly integrity and public engagement in hopes of arriving at a cooler, more captivating anthropology. What are some of the tensions of maintaining academic integrity while being guided by your own sociopolitical perspective?

3 VIP used ethnographic stories accompanied by photographs in order to grab viewers' attention. How do you decide which elements of an ethnographic story are compelling when you are curating your public scholarship?

4 Often, when undergraduates know that their writing and research will be accessible to wide audiences on the internet, students write stronger, more responsibly, and with greater enjoyment, regardless of what they write about. What are some ways to maintain academic rigor using this pedagogical writing strategy?

Figure 7.12. Residential yard art, East McDowell Road neighborhood, Phoenix, 2018.

ACKNOWLEDGMENTS

Visualizing Immigrant Phoenix would not exist without the many thousands of transnational migrants who have settled in Phoenix and put their distinctive imprint on the city. It is also indebted to the fabulous research, writing, and photography of the research team members, who documented some of the migrants' stories. All were undergraduates at Arizona State University during their participation in the project: Cynthia Canez, Crystal Cespedes, Jonnathan Flores, Christen Garden, José Grijalva, Yerena Hernandez, Argenis Hurtado Moreno, Patrick Ingham, Hussein Mohamed, Sanhareb Nano, Megan Reder, Nina Rocket, Chrystin Sanchez, and Ileen Younan. Their dedication, creativity, and delight in engaging with Phoenix's immigrant communities made this project truly a labor of love for us all. We are indebted to modest funding from ASU's New College of Interdisciplinary Arts through its far-sighted NCUIRE program. All photos taken by Koptiuch unless another team member is specified. We thank readers for perusing our website!

REFERENCES

Ahmed, Sara. 2010. "Happy Objects." In *The Affect Theory Reader*, ed. Melissa Gregg and Gregory J. Seigworth, 29–51. Durham: Duke University Press.

Barthes, Roland. 1971. "From Work to Text." In *Image, Music, Text*, trans. Stephen Heath, 155–64. New York: Hill and Wang.

De León, Jason. 2015. *The Land of Open Graves: Living and Dying on the Migrant Trail*. Berkeley: University of California Press.

Diaz, David R. 2005. *Barrio Urbanism: Chicanos, Planning, and American Cities*. New York: Routledge.

Diaz, David R., and Rodolfo D. Torres, eds. 2012. *Latino Urbanism: The Politics of Planning, Policy and Redevelopment*. New York: New York University Press.

Gonzalez, Erualdo R. 2017. *Latino City: Urban Planning, Politics, and the Grassroots*. New York: Routledge.

Koptiuch, Kristin. 2012. "Cruzando Fronteras/Crossing Phoenix." *Urban Vignettes*. https://www.academia.edu/5002386/Koptiuch_Cruzando _Fronteras_Crossing_Phoenix_2012.

Koptiuch, Kristin. 2017. "Visualizing Immigrant Youth in Phoenix." *Youth Circulations* (blog), July 8. http://www.youthcirculations.com/blog /2017/7/8/visualizingimmigrantphoenix.

Koptiuch, Kristin. 2019. "Taquerías Conversas: Latinx Immigrants Remake the Flickering Urban Landscape of Phoenix." *Entanglements* 2, no. 1: 76–96. https://entanglementsjournal.org/taquerias-conversas/.

Lara, Jesus J. 2018. *Latino Placemaking and Planning: Cultural Resilience and Strategies for Reurbanization*. Tucson: University of Arizona Press.

Rios, Michael, and Leonardo Vazquez, eds. 2012. *Diálogos: Placemaking in Latino Communities*. New York: Routledge.

Sandoval, Gerardo. 2009. *Immigrants and the Revitalization of Los Angeles: Development and Change in MacArthur Park*. Amherst: Cambria Press.

Sandoval-Strausz, A. 2019. *Latino Landscapes: How Latin American Immigrants Saved Urban America*. New York: Basic Books.

Valdez Moses, Michael. 2001. "Magical Realism at World's End." *Literary Imagination* 3, no. 1: 105–33. https://doi.org/10.1093/litimag/3.1.105.

CHAPTER EIGHT

The Tale Is the Map: Virtual Reality Experiences in Anthropology

R. Scott Wilson

When the virtual reality (VR) experience *We Live Here* (Troche 2019) begins, the viewer is with the main character, Rockey, inside the tent in which she has been living for several months as part of a large homeless encampment. As she tells the viewer about her recent experiences, the noise outside grows louder and louder. Opening the door to the tent, the viewer becomes aware that the Los Angeles Police Department and some sanitation workers are clearing the site. Within minutes, the police are leading Rockey away, telling her that she has to leave the majority of her possessions behind. Dismayed, she leaves with the police. The viewer is left behind, wondering what will become of her and where she will go. For clues, the viewer is offered the opportunity to look through some of the things she left behind – to find previous addresses and, maybe, the names of relatives or friends.

   Opening a nearby coffee can, I discover her cell phone, which she had been careful to hide from the police. I see a video message from her ex-husband, reminding her to contact him if she needs anything. Other items reveal other aspects of her story – from getting married on a motorcycle en route to Sturgis, South Dakota, to an animated sequence of her childhood dreams of being a cowboy. The viewer is allowed to literally walk around freely in her tent because the project features "roomscale" navigation, and manipulable objects light up when the viewer approaches. At the end of my exploration, Rockey returns and asks a series of questions about real-life situations that can leave a person at risk of being unhoused. It's a powerful, moving experience that left me in tears on my first viewing. I start by describing this project because of how it encapsulates so much of the potential for VR in anthropology. Rockey is a real person, and the artifacts that make up the film represent real pieces of her life – carefully and collaboratively curated to tell a new kind of immersive story. While this kind of project is beyond the technical and financial capabilities of most anthropology departments and individual anthropologists, it offers insights into what our goals should be in introducing this format into our ethnographic toolkit.

In this chapter I recount my experience in teaching about and producing short-form ethnographic 360 cinema from an anthropological perspective. I have found the experience intellectually rewarding and well worth the technological, financial, and institutional barriers I have encountered along the way. I narrate my earliest forays into the world of 360/VR ethnographic film and the particular challenges I and my students have had to overcome to produce my first feature-length production, *Birthplace of the People: A Tongva Origin Story*. In the first half of this chapter, I discuss the logistics of producing VR documentaries in a classroom setting. From technology to funding strategies, it has been a long and winding road to the present. In the second half of the chapter, I discuss the process of creating VR documentaries in the context of academic institutional constraints. My hope is that this chapter could be useful for those interested in exploring the utility of VR/360 video in their classes and/or research.

THE PATH TO VIRTUAL REALITY

My rationale for exploring VR as a mode of ethnographic presentation grew out of my New Media Ethnography course. Rather quickly, the course evolved into a seminar on spatial storytelling, with students constructing multi-linear documentaries that resembled different types of real-world spaces. Narratives, for example, could be made to follow the logics of places such as farmers' markets (non-sequential with a central node) or a natural history museum (linear with an endpoint, with opportunities to stop and explore along the way). New technologies offer opportunities to tell new kinds of human stories. Rather than using montage editing to construct a story-world across different times and locations, as is done in traditional documentaries, the world building of 360 video takes place within view of the camera, usually within one or two locations. As a result, the space itself becomes the subject of the film, with linear narrative yielding to mood, setting, atmosphere, and ambience. As Bailenson (2018) notes, VR/360 video seems designed to take people to places they would never go, to experience things they could never experience.

It dovetails nicely with the best kinds of classic ethnographic writings. The traditional anthropological focus on the "native's point of view" can be taken quite literally here, as the aim is to teleport the viewer to inhabit unfamiliar places, with unfamiliar people.

In this regard, it dovetails nicely with the best kinds of classic ethnographic writings. The traditional anthropological focus on the "native's point of view" can be taken quite literally here, as the aim is to teleport the viewer to inhabit unfamiliar places, with unfamiliar people.

Producing VR footage can get expensive, but there are relatively inexpensive ways to get started. One of the advantages of the VR film production process is that there is a major difference between VR production and traditional film production. Whereas traditional films require long periods of shooting, the bulk of the work in VR production goes toward planning.

Overall, the technical requirements for getting into VR production are similar to, and sometimes even more feasible than, traditional film. For less than $10,000, a department could create a professional-level production setup, even if it is just with one camera and one computer to start. Our department started with just that: one VR camera and one VR-ready computer in 2015. With that setup we were able to crank out enough projects to raise more funding. Eventually, we managed to collect enough VR equipment that storage became an issue. Our funding has been 100 percent internal at California State University–Long Beach, but it took some maneuvering to make that happen. Our efforts in VR started modestly; nonetheless, we were able to produce a solid slate of VR films in our first year, which was important for demonstrating its potential as a valid method for presenting ethnographic insights. This is the most important aspect of raising funding, whether it comes from the institution or from an external grant. In our case, establishing an institutional profile drew others from different departments and made collaborations with design, film, and journalism departments more feasible.

One suggestion for raising funds within the university would be to "make yourself useful." This has been our mantra for years in our department. As we started to collect videography equipment in our pre-VR years, we always made sure to stay on the dean's radar in terms of what we could offer the college and the university. Early on, we proposed making promotional videos for the college. These consisted of short, two- to three-minute promotional videos about students and faculty to be featured on university websites. They were not the most exciting projects for students to work on, but as our internal funding requests for lab equipment grew, our justifications became easier and easier.

PRODUCTION TIPS: PRESENCE AND EMPATHY

Early works in VR journalism like *Clouds Over Sidra* (2015) and Nonny de la Pena's *Hunger in Los Angeles* (2012) touched off an increased interest in the possibilities for VR in documentary circles. Best practices were (and still are) emergent, but two particular concepts became touchstones for producing stories in this mode: *presence* and *empathy*. Together, these two aspects of VR documentary are the most powerful arguments for integrating these methods into visual anthropology. Anthropologists have spent the past century sharpening their writing skills in order to give readers a sensory-filled experience of a location they have never visited. Photography, film, and video added two-dimensional, then moving, images and sound to fortify our ethnographic recreations. VR/360 video pushes this even further by immersing the viewer in three-dimensional spaces and soundscapes.

Presence refers to the sense of "being there" afforded by the fact that the viewer is located inside the space of the story – as if in the center of an image (either flat or in stereoscopic 3D). This refers to more than just placing a camera in a room as if it were an all-seeing security camera. Care must be taken to position the viewer in a way that the viewer experiences a sense of engagement with the world (and people) around them in the film.

Upon starting the VR production section of my class, once we have gone over using the camera, tripods, and microphones, I like to begin by asking the class a very simple question: "If you were making a VR film about this class discussion, where would you put the camera?" Almost invariably, the first student to answer will say, "in the middle of the table, of course. That way you can see everyone's faces, and record the whole scene without missing anything." The answer to the question, at least in terms of best practices, is that the camera should be in what I like to call a "human position." This means placing the camera in the position normally occupied by a person's head at a height that approximates an "average" person for the age group represented. The viewer will not be able to see everyone in the room clearly, but that's the point. In real life, this would be true as well.

When we create 360 experiences, we are not trying to replicate the world in its entirety; rather, we are recreating the world to simulate human perspectives. This is a fine distinction and a simple practice, but it makes all the difference in creating immersive, engaging experiences. If you want someone to feel as if they are "there," then their sensory experience should mirror the experience of being there, flaws and all.

> **When we create 360 experiences, we are not trying to replicate the world in its entirety; rather, we are recreating the world to simulate human perspectives.... If you want someone to feel as if they are "there," then their sensory experience should mirror the experience of being there, flaws and all.**

Presence is critical in VR filmmaking; however, *empathy* is the more frequently discussed term in this pair. *Empathy* refers to the supposed ability of virtual reality films to facilitate an empathetic, emotional bond between viewer and subject. This bond can motivate people, it is said, to support a political cause, join a movement, donate to a human rights organization, or even shift their views on policy. This is a worthy goal, but most accounts of empathy in the realm of VR fail to discuss *how* empathy is achieved in these contexts. It is as if the assumption is that the VR platform itself will automatically *create* empathy for the people featured in the video. I am not sure that this is the case, but it's a worthy goal. My only suggestion here is to follow the lead of the people in the film in terms of what matters and what should be the focus. This should always be the animating focus of your team's collaborations.

PRODUCTION TIPS: THE USE OF SPACE

As with traditional filmmaking, the process of producing VR films can be divided into three phases: preproduction, production, and postproduction. However, unlike traditional videography, the most work-intensive phase in VR filmmaking is preproduction. This surprises most students in the course, as many of them come in with a moderate amount of filmmaking experience. Rather than long, extended shoots followed by tedious stints at the editing station, VR filmmaking usually consists of copious amounts of conceptualizing and design followed by a relatively quick burst of shooting and then a relatively simple round of editing. Design, then, takes the forefront in VR production, and it is what makes ethnographic VR so engaging. In this section, I will cover what we've learned about the preproduction, production, and post-production processes.

The first step in VR filmmaking is to ask one simple question: Does the film need to be a VR/360 production? Bailenson discusses this at length, and I agree with his conclusion that not all projects are suited to the VR format. To tell a compelling story in VR, there needs to be a substantial spatial component – that is, the space needs to be part of the story. The spatial dimension needs to have a considerable impact on the story you want to tell and should offer additional information about the subjects of the film or the event you are intending to capture. Once the students have formed production groups of three to four students based on mutual interest in a topic, I immediately ask them whether their project is suited for VR. If, for example, their "elevator pitch" sounds like a story that could easily be told via interviews, or that would need to take place in multiple locations, I encourage them to either rethink the topic or choose another one. The most success-ful projects in the New Media Ethnography class have been ones that were grounded in particular spaces, whether those spaces were real, imagined, or a combination of the two. But this is only possible if the team engages in design principles rooted in ethnographic research. Two films from the early years of the course can serve as examples of how ethnographic VR filmmakers can recreate virtual spaces to tell real human stories.

Perception was a three-minute student film that introduces the viewer to Anthony, a recent university student who had lost his sight at a young age due to retinitis pigmentosa. As Anthony explains through voiceover, his world is not completely black. He can perceive spaces and some colors, and he uses these abilities to navigate social situations alongside his other senses. It is a complicated picture, and film director Jinny Choe spent hours interviewing Anthony about his experiences. Eventually they collaborated to design the experiences as part profile/part simulator. Halfway through the film, the viewer's perspective shifts from third person to first person. As Anthony describes his experiences, the color and some focus begin to fade from the viewer's perception. It is subtle at first – a few viewers even thought that there was a malfunction – but eventually the viewer is seeing Anthony's world in a way that approximates his detailed descriptions from the preproduction interviews. His voiceover remains as a guide, but both the sense of presence and empathy for Anthony's situation are rendered in multiple dimensions.

Perception is an excellent example of using interview data to build a virtual world for the viewer. The key shot from the project focuses on a red Stanford University water bottle as the other colors fade away – illustrating Anthony's statement that bright red is the only color that he can vividly make out (see Figure 8.1). At the end of the film as well, the viewer's world morphs into the shapes, patterns, and hues that make up his visual world, replicating his particular sensual perception in 360 video.

Another example resulted from my own collaboration with students in the course. *The Body of Prix* recounts a former member of the Mormon church's struggle to reclaim her own sense of bodily independence. Her chosen platform to pursue this project has been to perform as a professional burlesque artist. I first heard of her story because of her final project performance in another of my classes, Encounters and Identities. She had performed a short striptease for the class and given a lecture on how her chosen career in burlesque was also a project of self-discovery and resistance. After class, I immediately asked her if she would like to collaborate on a VR film about her story, and she agreed. What drew me to the story as a potential VR film was that she talked about her interactions with the audience, and how those interactions shaped her own sense of herself as a gendered and sexual being at any given moment during each performance. The space of the stage and the physical contact between herself and the audience members, according to her own account, merged to produce a shifting,

Figure 8.1. Still from *Perception* (2018).

multifaceted, and unpredictable persona on stage: Prix de Beauté. The six-minute performance, set to Vidmar Berlin-style cabaret music, consists of Natalie transforming herself from a roaring twenties styled dandy gentleman complete with mustache, cane, and pinstripe suit to a glamorous femme feather dancer. After much teasing and audience interaction, the feathers fall away.

The first step, again, is the interview process. We recorded two hours of interviews and used the recordings to design the world of the film. Her transformation from Natalie to Prix takes place in a series of spaces – from parking lot to dressing room to stage – and we wanted the viewer to accompany her on her performative journey. For the dressing room scene, we positioned the camera over her shoulder (see Figure 8.2) so that the viewer can watch her apply the eye lashes, blush, and other accoutrements that she uses in her transformation. The props that decorate the dressing room space are gradually applied to the body that becomes the focus for the entire show to come, and this first scene offers the viewer an opportunity to see the makeup, feathers, eyelashes, and mustache – the tools she uses to play with gender during the performance.

The remainder of the film consists of her six-minute performance shot from three different angles. Since everything is on camera during a VR shoot, we had her perform the routine three times, with the camera in three different locations – two times from the front row of the audience, and one angle from the back of the stage. We wanted the viewer to take the position of an audience member so that they could see both the performance and the reactions of the other audience members nearby. In postproduction, we edited the three performances together with as few cuts as possible – giving it the appearance of a multi-camera production. As with all VR shoots, the production required much collaboration between filmmakers and subject, and we discussed her stage location and audience interactions at length before beginning.

Birthplace of the People: A Tongva Origin Story is a 14-minute 360 virtual reality film that tells the Tongva/Gabrieliño story of Wiyat and the birth of the Tongva people on the site of Puvungna, which now includes California State University's Long Beach (CSULB) campus. Puvungna – which means place of the great gathering – was the site of the world's creation but also its first death and funeral. This 360-degree VR experience immerses the viewer in the spiritual place of Los

Figure 8.2 Still from *The Body of Prix* (2019).

Angeles' original inhabitants – in a mythological space that transcends time. By connecting this physical place to its spiritual past, the film is intended to remind us of histories we may have either forgotten or may have never known. The film is narrated by Tongva CSULB faculty member Cindi Alvitre, and visual artist Carly Lake produced the artwork using the Tilt Brush VR 3D art program (see Figure 8.3). The viewer's perspective is guided by a VR camera that takes a slow path through Lake's 3D renderings of scenes in Alvitre's narration, animated using the video game authoring software Unity.

Much like our other projects, this film began with an interview with Alvitre about the significance of the site and how the Tongva/ Gabrieliño community understands its place in the world. We had originally planned to do a regular VR documentary, but early in the process it became clear to both of us that it would be more powerful if we literally transported people to the mythical time described in the mythology. To do this, we would have to recreate the space as described in the story. The intent was to immerse the viewer in an overlay that depicts the spiritual world on top of the physical one, and we managed to do that with Lake's artwork, a soundscape corresponding with narrated events, and music from a group of Tongva singers.

Birthplace also represents one of the most important aspects of authoring VR content: collaboration. The concept that Alvitre and I developed required skills and knowledges that exceeded the two of us. Alvitre and Lake had previously collaborated on a children's book, and I managed to recruit graduate students who I knew were familiar with Unity for animating the VR camera. My role as director was to bring people together and to put them in a position to do what they do best.

THE FUTURE

One describes a tale best by telling the tale. You see? The way one describes a story, to oneself or to the world, is by telling the story. It is a balancing act and it is a dream. The more accurate the map, the more it resembles the territory. The most accurate map possible would be the territory, and thus would be perfectly accurate and perfectly useless.

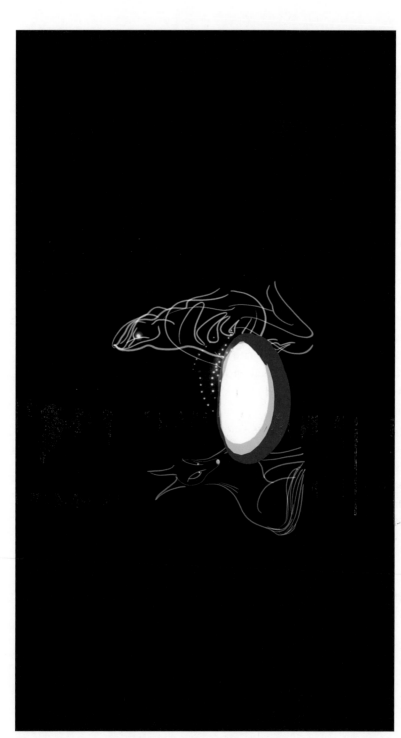

Figure 8.3. Scene detail featuring "Coyote" and "Red-Legged Frog Woman" from the VR film *Birthplace of the People* (2020). Tilt Brush art by Carly Lake.

The tale is the map that is the territory.

You must remember this.

– Neil Gaiman, American Gods

I use this quote in the introductory meeting of my New Media Ethnography class to spur conversations about the role of new media technologies in producing visual ethnographies. More specifically, I use it to highlight how visual (and I would argue, all) ethnographies are creative endeavors. The goal is not to recreate a completely accurate version of the world around us, but to create a heightened, sensation-filled version of that world that can illustrate what matters vis-à-vis the people featured in the production.

Our goal with these projects is to document and create representations of the world around us, but also to collaborate with the subjects of our films to create new ways of imagining the spaces around us. VR/360 video offers an opportunity for us to work together with various communities and peoples to build virtual worlds for audiences to inhabit.

In that sense, our goal with these projects is to document and create representations of the world around us, but also to collaborate with the subjects of our films to create new ways of imagining the spaces around us. VR/360 video offers an opportunity for us to work together with various communities and peoples to build virtual worlds for audiences to inhabit.

Moving into the future, I feel pretty fortunate and excited, from both practical and conceptual standpoints. There really aren't that many technical hurdles to overcome in producing 360 videos, now that the technologies needed to do it are relatively mainstream and inexpensive. Bringing VR into classrooms is becoming more and more feasible, and it would allow students to build marketable skills to add to their CVs and resumes. Many nonprofits, media outlets, and marketing firms look for students with production experience, and more and more of them are interested in creating VR and interactive content and promotional materials. During the global pandemic, for example, museums around the world frantically created virtual tours of their collections that patrons and potential donors could visit remotely. Several of my former students found themselves doing this and contacted me about how excited they were to be working in VR again.

The bigger hurdle at the moment is probably the institutional barriers that make visual anthropology a risky endeavor for junior faculty. In our department, we decided about 10 years ago to alter our department tenure policy to incorporate visual work alongside written publications. The institutional practice of "making yourself useful" to various deans and administrators may involve some extra work – producing profile pieces takes time and is not always that interesting. However, becoming the college's or university's promotional firm pays off in the end by highlighting the value of visual storytelling to a wider audience, and this can make a fairly substantial difference in how VR ethnographies are interpreted by colleagues who will make funding and curricular decisions around the university.

Another area that needs development is the distribution of VR projects outside of traditional academic settings. An increasingly public anthropology demands that those of us working in the field of new media find ways to overcome the technological and institutional barriers to bringing these projects to an outside audience. VR headsets have become less expensive in recent years but are still not considered a mainstream household item – unlike video game consoles or smart televisions. But there are still a few ways to display these projects in a public setting, sharing our work with those who have helped us create them.

In our first two years of VR production, we used the Samsung Gear smartphone-based headsets to show our projects on campus and at our annual off-campus film festival. This was convenient to an extent, but we were always reliant on the number of smartphones available via myself and several students. A better solution emerged with the Oculus Go headset – which, along with the Google Daydream, represented the first mobile, high-quality stand-alone headset. These were indispensable at film festivals and conferences in that films could be sideloaded onto them very quickly and they were infinitely portable. The Oculus Quest takes these assets even further, offering "six degrees of freedom" (roomscale capabilities) and even higher quality in addition to portability.

More recently, however, the Gerald M. Kline Innovation Space on campus at CSULB unveiled a virtual reality theater, in which I was able to display *Birthplace of the People* during our February 2020 World Anthropology Day festivities. The theater allowed 20 viewers per session and was an effective means of allowing a group of viewers to experience the film simultaneously. In addition, we were able to invite Tongva community members to experience the film together and to take the position of a passenger traveling through representations of the story they had shared with us. The traditional experience of engaging in a film as part of a group is important, one that I hope will become more common moving forward.

I should mention that not all innovations in anthropological VR are due to technological advancements. Sometimes we have to reach back in the technological timeline and adapt to the conditions with which we are presented. After the campus shut down due to the COVID-19 pandemic in March 2020, my collaborators and I received a grant from the Los Angeles County Department of Arts and Culture. The grant was to feature the film as part of a larger ceremony to commemorate the removal of the Columbus statue in front of Los Angeles City Hall, in Grant Park. The organizers wanted to feature our film in the festivities, but the ongoing pandemic made the use of regular headsets impossible. Instead, one of the event organizers that worked for Los Angeles County suggested that we make use of Google Cardboard headsets, which were one of the first available means for people to experience VR, debuting in 2014. This was a step back in terms of technology, but it was the perfect solution in the age of the pandemic.

We ended up distributing Cardboard headsets – featuring art from the film and a QR code for launching it in the mobile YouTube app. Event participants were each given a headset (they cost $6 to $7 to print from various vendors) that they could use with their own mobile devices. We printed 300 of the headsets and distributed about 100 at the event. The other 200 were strategically placed at libraries, tribal community centers, and museums all over Los Angeles County. The county also soon placed an additional order and has distributed a further 300. Our hope is that children, teachers, and their families can also take the trip to the Puvungna as it exists in the tales of the ancestors and survives in the tellings of contemporary orators, by using their own mobile devices.

The possibilities are nearly endless when it comes to how VR can be used in the service of traditional anthropological goals. The project *We Live Here* – with its roomscale interactivity – is the next level on my personal journey of VR creation. I can only imagine how powerful an ethnographic VR film featuring artifacts, ritual para-phernalia, or other material culture items that the viewer could interact with could be. But with collaboration and experimentation, we could be ready to make something similar fairly soon. All it takes is to recognize a situation or scene that would be a fitting experience for an uninitiated viewer – then composing the situation as a VR experience. Once that comes together, it is only a matter of collaborating with the film subjects to plan the tableau or scene and recruiting the right production team to piece it together. The future is bright for VR in anthropology, and I look forward to seeing where my fellow anthropologists take it.

FOR DISCUSSION

1 VR video offers new opportunities to curate, organize, and present the materials that traditionally constitute ethnographic data. What are some of these new opportunities and how do they add to the stories we tell?

2 VR films and traditional documentaries provide different opportunities and limitations in production and dissemination. For which stories, spaces, and audiences would each of these modalities be most useful?

3 "Making yourself useful" is an effective way to raise funding both within the university and in the surrounding community. In which ways could an emerging multimedia production outfit benefit the university/institution/organization *and* surrounding communities?

4 Space is central when producing VR cinema. What does it mean to say that "the space needs to be part of the story"?

5 Anthropologists have much to gain from collaborating with graphic designers, web designers, and artists. With who else and in what other ways could we collaborate as we create ethnographically rich virtual worlds for viewers to inhabit?

REFERENCES

Bailenson, Jeremy. 2018. *Experience on Demand: What Virtual Reality Is, How It Works, and What It Can Do.* New York: W.W. Norton & Company.

de la Peña, Nonny, dir. 2012. *Hunger in Los Angeles.* MIT – Docubase.

Milk, Chris, and Gabo Arora, dir. 2015. *Clouds Over Sidra.* Produced in partnership with the United Nations and Samsung.

Troche, Rose. 2019. *We Live Here.* VR for Good/Invisible People. Available as an app through Oculus.

CHAPTER NINE

Creating Inclusive Public Space: Participatory Design Ethnography in a University Library

Krista M. Harper, Sarah C. Hutton, Vanesa Giraldo Gartner,
Elena Sesma, Castriela Hernández-Reyes, and Caitlin Homrich-Knieling

University libraries serve the public every day as they adapt to broad social, institutional, and technological transformations in higher education. With the advent of the internet and mobile computing, higher education and academic libraries have become inextricably intertwined with technology. Over the past 25 years, documents have been transformed from paper to digital objects hosted on a network; this rapid digital shift has the influence to change everything else in higher education and in the academic library as well (Lewis 2016). As a result of this digital transformation, academic libraries have been experiencing transformations of their own.

Libraries have three core purposes:

1 maintaining materials and documents long term
2 providing knowledge and resources to communities
3 helping individuals to locate and use information

These functions look far different today than they did even just five years ago (Lewis 2016). Public higher education libraries serve a wider range of patrons than ever before in terms of race, ethnicity, gender, nationality, age, sexual orientation, disability status, and more (US Department of Education 2017). Since the 1990s, there have been multiple calls to recruit people of color into librarianship (Jennings 1993), but the profession still does not reflect the diversity of library users (Jones and Murphy 2019). Addressing the social and technological transformations that contemporary academic libraries now face requires a stronger focus on user experience, space navigation and preference, and service expectations. Libraries have typically relied on traditional quantitative methodologies, such as tracking collection use, to make decisions about service and space planning. Higher education libraries are now seeking out partnerships with anthropologists as experts in ethnographic research methods.

THE LIBRARY NEEDS ANTHROPOLOGY!

Though studying one's own university library may seem prosaic compared to the field sites regularly featured in the ethnographies we read in anthropology classes, it is just as essential for fostering an understanding of the world around us. Over the past few decades, academic libraries have faced dramatic changes in order to adapt to new forms of production, distribution, and consumption of information by their patrons. Our own public research university library is open 24 hours a day on weekdays, plus weekend hours, and thousands of students and community members visit each day. Over the course of 2016, the university library had 1,762,263 visitors. What are they all doing? Who is there at 4 am? How do they experience the library?

Our research touches upon practical design concerns, such as how students perceive and use built space, technology, and library services like the website. We have also pursued questions related to students' motivations for using the library and how emotions of anxiety, exclusion, belonging, and comfort shape the student experience.

Our research touches upon practical design concerns, such as how students perceive and use built space, technology, and library services like the website. We have also pursued questions related to students' motivations for using the library and how emotions of anxiety, exclusion, belonging, and comfort shape the student experience.

Since the library employs over a hundred public workers and hundreds of student staff, we are interested in understanding how the design of spaces and workflows shapes how employees experience the library as a public service workplace.

The University of Massachusetts Amherst Libraries comprise a public space within a larger public university. In light of broader national and university-wide discussions about how to foster an inclusive campus climate, we investigated how students express a sense of identity and belonging in university and library spaces, with attention to the experiences of students of color, international students, LGBTQ+ students, those returning, and first-generation students. As we developed our research project on the W.E.B. Du Bois Library campus public space, student researchers attended a series of forums related to issues faced by students of color and other underrepresented groups on campus, like name-calling and microaggressions in residential halls and inequitable access to campus facilities and services. Student government representatives elevated student demands for attention to classroom experiences of racism and the need for outreach in local communities of color. The Campus Climate Survey (University of Massachusetts Amherst 2017) further documented these problems and contributed new knowledge about the experiences of first-generation students and LGBTQ+ students, faculty, and staff. Research by Katapol (2010) suggests that students of color may experience heightened anxiety with respect to using resources and interacting with library staff. Other research has demonstrated, however, that the library serves a critical role as a "third space" that supports students from underrepresented and/or marginalized populations (Codispoti and Frey 2007). With increased awareness of how library staff, services, and spaces could impact the university experience for many members of these groups, the library had an opportunity to foster and share havens for academic success.

In 2013, UMass librarians Sarah Hutton and Carol Will contacted Krista Harper (anthropologist), saying "The library needs anthropology!" Harper answered their call, and thus the Library Transformations Project was born. Since Spring 2014, Harper has trained nine class teams of undergraduate and graduate students in qualitative research techniques and led them in data collection with the goal of understanding how students and other members of the campus community perceive and experience the university library.[1] Harper has now led

---

[1] Anthropology professors Art Keene and Amanda Walker Johnson also contributed student research to the libraries in Spring 2013 and Spring 2015.

over 90 undergraduate and graduate student researchers through the process of conducting a qualitative research project for the W.E.B. Du Bois Library's Learning Commons, working closely with librarians. In particular, the research teams were tasked with studying how different members of the diverse undergraduate student body experience the library as a space: Is it comfortable and inclusive? Are there spaces that students perceive as unwelcoming? How do undergraduates find support and a place where they can feel productive?

The research has expanded from its initial focus on students' study habits and spaces to investigate broader questions of students' experiences of identity, belonging (and exclusion), and academic support. The student research presented consists of two distinct parts. First, we sought to learn about students' academic experiences on the UMass campus and how these shape their experiences of the library specifically. The second part of our research sought to understand how students with varied identities and experiences perceive the library as a space that helps or hinders their academic success. We found that while a few students expressed signs of "library anxiety" (Gremmels 2015), many students from historically underrepresented groups saw the library as a haven and found ways to create a sense of community and comfort within the library (Jiao, Onwuegbuzie, and Bostick 2004; Codispoti and Frey 2007). Gaining an understanding of these students' practices and perceptions could yield insights for improving the library as a campus "third space."

DEPLOYING PARTICIPATORY DESIGN ETHNOGRAPHY

Our participatory design ethnography collaboration is successful because it integrates real-life organizational research into a qualitative research methods curriculum that is regularly offered by the Department of Anthropology and the School of Public Policy. Each year, undergraduate and graduate students in these courses generate new research questions and foci, as participant-researchers who simultaneously draw upon their own experiences as students at the university and their emerging knowledge of ethnographic and participatory action research (PAR) methods. Each student cohort builds upon the knowledge base of previous cohorts, and after five years of the Library Transformations Project, we have developed strong partnerships with the university library's administration and workers.

Student researchers have intensively studied the W.E.B. Du Bois Library's Learning Commons, located just steps from their classroom. As a major service area for students and residents of the Commonwealth of Massachusetts, the Learning Commons integrates many library and academic services into a shared space. Numerous library departments are stakeholders in the successful implementation of services for patrons; library user data has implications not only for how spaces are populated, but also for how library resources and services are accessed and used. Trends identified by research in this highly trafficked area therefore have implications for how the libraries make strategic investments in collections, staff positions, and technologies, and these strategic decisions stretch beyond library walls into the campus community.

Not only is the library centrally located on campus, but at UMass Amherst, the W.E.B. Du Bois Library plays a central role in the campus academic success ecosystem as well. Librarians sit on multiple faculty councils, weaving critical digital literacy imperatives into the curriculum, alongside faculty partners. The library has partnered with myriad programs including the International Programs Office, Financial Aid, and the Writing Center, all of which have physical operations space in the Learning Commons. With this high concentration of students, faculty, and staff in a centralized location, the library is ripe with opportunities for student researchers. Given the high number of collaborative partnerships across departments, programs, and divisions, the research findings are of interest to stakeholders across the university.

As we embarked on our ethnography of an academic library, we looked to the work of design ethnographers for guidance. Two works by anthropologist-librarian teams, Foster and Gibbons's *Studying Students* (2007) and Duke and Asher's *College Libraries and Student Culture: What We Now Know* (2012), offered us concrete models for carrying out ethnographic research in a university library. We also drew upon the expertise of Donna Lanclos, who has been writing about library anthropology and user experience (UX) since 2010 on her blog, *The Anthropologist in the Stacks,* and in her published research (Lanclos 2016; Lanclos and Asher 2016). Studying library spaces meant we needed to brush up on our design thinking. Fortunately, the work of design anthropologist

Dori Tunstall was there for us (2013), and we also drew upon the ideas in design scholar Dan Lockton's *Design with Intent Method* (2010) to develop our own insights about the intersection of design and social behavior in academic libraries.

Drawing on principles of participatory design and applied anthropology, students conducted interviews and participant observation, organized and carried out three Photovoice focus group sessions, and documented and analyzed their data. Using different methods allowed us to capture students' stories about and perceptions of the library, as well as knowledge gaps, emplaced routines, and embodied practices that they might have found difficult to articulate verbally. Walking interviews and participant observation provided the bulk of the data. Participant observation was conducted in the Learning Commons and other library spaces with additional observations at public events on campus.

Through a collective process informed by Ryan and Bernard's (2003) discussion of how to identify themes, the research team created a codebook that included both top-down codes based on the interview questions and also open codes based on participant observation and in vivo coding of interview transcripts (Galman 2016). Once condensed and grouped by theme, the "codebook" was imported into QDA software. Following this group coding process, we ran queries of the data regarding identity, belonging, community, and social interactions in the library and were able to draw out and develop repetitive themes in the data as well as discern themes that occurred only rarely (Ryan and Bernard 2003). At the end of the semester, students compiled and wrote up their results, then gave formal presentations of their findings to an audience of over 20 UMass librarians, including the library dean.

BELONGING

Our research project shed light on the many features that draw students to the library and that support students' needs. Students who frequently use the library come for a variety of reasons: convenient printing, group study spaces, and individual work spaces surrounded by other students. They come because their friends come to the library or they have no home study space, or because the library puts them into the right mindset for work. Kira, an African-American student, told a student researcher, "I feel like when I want to learn or do anything academic, being in a place where that's the focus helps me…. And it's what this is." Lourdes, a Latina undergraduate student, was drawn to the library not only for studying, but also for public events and socializing:

> I've come to some talks. I've participated in two, one about jazz,
> and one about wild animals … I've come to print, to attend meet-
> ings, and I've used the coffee area. I meet my classmates there, and
> we talk and we eat.

Functionally, the library is a free, public, multipurpose space that bridges students' social and academic lives.

Themes that emerged from the data included students' desire for belonging in the library. Students saw two different kinds of library spaces as promoting a stronger sense of belonging: spaces that created a sense of community through design features and activities, and spaces that reduced students' anxious experience of "not knowing" where to seek resources and support.

Themes related to "not knowing" how to get library services and resources emerged from participant observation in the library and also at the campus listening sessions, which generated awareness that a variety of students experience a sense of exclusion on campus. One participant, Carla, said that she sometimes felt marginalized as the only first-generation Latina student in her classes. Carla had hoped to find a sense of belonging in the Learning Commons based on her positive childhood experiences of her town library. Instead, she found it overwhelming and off-putting: "Yeah, it just seems a little bit like an intimidating space sometimes when you come down here, which might be my own fault." Alicia, an international student from Latin America, expressed frustration with navigating the library:

> [The] library is the most complex resource in any university. There
> are many pathways, many steps, many rules, and many concepts
> in the library, so learning how to use it is difficult. I would like to
> understand how to use it overnight, but it's not possible.

Students' descriptions of the library's most high-traffic service areas demonstrated that the library needed to streamline wayfinding and provide a "one-stop shopping" service area in the Learning Commons so that patrons are less overwhelmed.

Some spaces in the library, however, seemed to allow students to create a sense of ownership over them by regularly working and socializing there. One researcher studied how students use the twenty-second floor East Asian Studies area. The books in the stacks and the signs in the reading room are in Japanese, Chinese, and Korean, and there is a staircase mural based on themes in Asian art. One can hear students speaking Chinese in the language tutoring room, throughout the halls, and in the reading room on the twenty-second floor. Language tutors, many of whom are international students, formed friendships and a sense of belonging in the library through the tutoring room. They spent their afternoons doing homework together, socializing, and tutoring students who came for help and practice. The fact that Chinese and other languages were spoken freely and loudly on the twenty-second floor was positive recognition of students' linguistic identity, institutionalized with a space in the library, and contrasted with the stigma that Chinese speakers experienced elsewhere on campus. Students were also drawn to the reading and tutoring rooms for their large laptop tables, comfy chairs, and designated space for studying and socializing.

Beyond the East Asian Studies area, our team identified other spaces and student practices that generated a sense of being at home on campus. Manuel, a Latino student, expressed his enthusiasm for the Learning Commons Microclimate, an area where librarians test out a variety of new furnishings:

> I think the space, the fact that it's a new space, has to do with it, because right when it was created, my friend and I immediately went to it, like, "This is fun. We gotta make this ours."

The Microclimate is by its nature an "experimental" study space, with an ever-changing array of sectional sofas, diner booths, futuristic egg-shaped chairs, and cylindrical study cubicles. Manuel's comment helped the librarians see it was exactly this slightly chaotic, unfinished quality of the Microclimate that felt open and inviting for some students.

Interview participants often referred to the W.E.B. Du Bois Library as a central landmark of the UMass Amherst campus, and one international student from Africa shared their sense of pride in looking up at the 26-story building and knowing that it was named after an African-American scholar who was born in western Massachusetts and went on to have global influence as a social scientist and activist. At the time of our study, the University Libraries were launching a new W.E.B. Du Bois Center, housing the W.E.B. Du Bois archives as well as resources and programming related to issues of race, labor, and social justice. The space allocated for the center had previously housed a related archive with filing cabinets and bookcases, but it had no public meeting space. The Library Transformations research team worked with the director, Professor Whitney Battle-Baptiste, to understand how to make the space more visible and relevant to students. Under her leadership, the W.E.B. Du Bois Center has come alive as a new academic space with conference tables, an exhibition area, public study hours, and regular programming, including a "Mondays with Du Bois" reading group where students, faculty, and community members discuss a reading by Du Bois and materials from the Du Bois archives.

COLLABORATION

Many invested stakeholders have made the Library Transformations Project a success. Harper's two departments, Anthropology and Public Policy, supported the continuity of the project by offering her qualitative research courses on an annual basis, allowing her to integrate teaching and research. Dean of Libraries Simon Neame, Library Director Emeritus Jay Schafer, and Associate Dean Leslie Button championed our student-focused research. Librarians Carol Will and Jennifer Friedman have worked to incorporate the Library Transformations Project into the library's overall planning process. Librarians and library staff regularly attended student presentations every semester and have been incredibly interested in and supportive of the ethnographic research course. Funding to cover participant costs was obtained via library administrative support and the application of successfully acquired faculty funds through the Massachusetts Society of Professors, the UMass Amherst Center for Teaching, and the UMass Amherst Campus Climate Improvement initiative.

Given the immediate applicability of this research to making improvements in the library, this collaboration has gained a fair amount of recognition across the UMass Amherst campus and beyond. Additionally, the accessible and scalable nature of this project has made it extremely attractive to academic

A participatory research methods course partnership is much more attainable to a broader population.

institutions of varying size and composition; while larger-scale collaborative library-anthropology research endeavors like ERIAL (Ethnographic Research in Illinois Academic Libraries) may be attractive, they are cost prohibitive to many under-resourced academic institutions. A participatory research methods course partnership is much more attainable to a broader population.

University librarians have already started to put student ethnographers' research into practice, integrating students' findings into the redesign of the Learning Commons and the W.E.B. Du Bois Center. Built in 2005, the Learning Commons at the W.E.B. Du Bois Library has long served as an exemplary model for other institutions seeking to develop a similar setup in their own libraries or learning centers. However, as it neared its tenth anniversary, it was clear to the director of libraries, Jay Schafer, that the Learning Commons was in dire need of transformative renovations in order for the libraries to continue to meet the needs of incoming and future students. The Learning Commons Assessment Task Force (LCATF) was formed to provide recommendations on facilities, service, and technology updates for a total transformation of the Learning Commons.

Anthropology students provided the university library with the qualitative data that librarians needed in order to discover how students use the Learning Commons space, services, and technology. While they had long been collecting ample quantitative data, the rich narratives provided by student ethnographers complemented the library's ongoing assessment to help complete the picture. Their research gave insights into student attitudes and perceptions in a way that would have been difficult for librarians to do on their own.

CONSTRAINTS AND APPLICATIONS

As anthropologists working on the design of existing public infrastructure, we have had to learn about working with hard constraints. In a 26-floor library, space must be set aside for elevators and stairs. Some of the library's toughest problems are literally concrete: the library has thick concrete walls and floors that are impossible to move and difficult even to drill through to make room for electric and ethernet cables. Student participants and researchers often have suggestions for improving the library that would require knocking it down and starting over fresh, which is not feasible for the foreseeable future.

What may be easier to change is the use of existing spaces and the model for organizing library services. Changing these, too, poses challenges for ethnographers. Higher education libraries are complex organizations. To students and faculty who use the library as patrons, the library is a service provider and public campus space. The library is also a workplace for over 200 people, and any changes to improve services and spaces affect the working conditions and even career trajectories of the people employed there. The Library Transformations Project therefore must be informed by action-research workplace ethnography as well as design ethnography approaches.

Findings from the student projects were almost immediately applicable in some cases. Our team pinpointed areas and services associated with the "not knowing" theme, allowing the library to improve wayfinding in high-traffic areas, one of the main sources of "library anxiety" in students.

Our research gave insights on how to reduce conflictual interactions between students in negotiating study spaces, a dynamic that contributed to anxiety and avoidance for some users. For example, on finding that students were confused about how to gain fair access to the group study rooms, librarians deployed an online reservation system that now allows students the ability to book rooms on their own without infringing upon others.

The Library Transformations Project also demonstrated students' desire for spaces that foster a sense of belonging, ownership, and identity. In libraries across the country, there is a strong push for sleek spaces that can be flexibly rearranged for different purposes. While this may be an efficient use of space, students still need fixed reference points, services, and features like artwork to generate positive feelings of place attachment.

Our team witnessed the alchemy of these elements in the East Asian Studies area, a place that fostered a strong sense of comfort and belonging for its users. In other semesters, we observed students "finding their space" in the Digital Media Lab and the W.E.B. Du Bois Center, underscoring the need for welcoming, dynamic library spaces and programs that serve the diverse constituencies of students that attend a public research university (Harper et al. 2016).

We learned firsthand how student ethnographers can contribute to more user-focused design that helps connect students with the resources they need to succeed.

Working together, we learned firsthand how student ethnographers can contribute to more user-focused design that helps connect students with the resources they need to succeed.

Student researchers in the Library Transformations Project have studied the most high-traffic, beating heart of campus – the largest part of the largest public university in Massachusetts. Their work shows how students can use applied anthropology in service of the public good (Foster 2015) and how ethnographic methods can be used to create inclusivity and belonging in public spaces on and off campus.

FOR DISCUSSION

1 This project had a strong focus on studying users' experience of a specific place that many people take for granted – the library. How has your anthropological lens helped you understand a common space or practice in a different way?

2 The student research team worked with librarians to develop a research design that integrated their questions and concerns about the transformations and challenges facing twenty-first-century higher education libraries. Why does the library need anthropology? How would other public spaces benefit from this type of project?

3 In the Library Transformations Project, ethnographers were interested in understanding how students of color experienced the library and especially which spaces felt welcoming or alienating to them. The team analyzed participant observation fieldnotes, Photovoice focus group discussions, and interviews to address these questions.

In considering equity and efficacy, how do you decide which methods best suit your project?
4 Using ethnography to assess how space is used is increasingly popular. What kinds of constraints do design ethnographers face in developing recommendations based on users' experience of the built environment?

ACKNOWLEDGMENTS

Parts of this chapter were previously published in the introduction to the September 2016 issue of *Anthro/Zine* (Harper et al. 2016).

REFERENCES

Codispoti, M., and S. Frey. 2007. "The Library as Third Place in Academe: Fulfilling a Need for Community in the Digital Age." Popular Culture & American Culture Association Annual National Conference, April 4–7, Boston, MA.

Duke, L.M., and A.D. Asher. 2012. *College Libraries and Student Culture: What We Now Know.* Chicago: American Library Association.

Foster, N.F. 2015. "Participatory Design for the Common Good." In *Participatory Visual and Digital Research in Action*, ed. A. Gubrium, K. Harper, and M. Otañez, 229–42. Walnut Creek: Left Coast Press.

Foster, N.F., and S.L. Gibbons. 2007. *Studying Students: The Undergraduate Research Project at the University of Rochester.* Chicago: American Library Association.

Galman, S.C. 2016. *The Good, the Bad, and the Data: Shane the Lone Ethnographer's Basic Guide to Qualitative Data Analysis.* New York: Routledge.

Gremmels, G.S. 2015. "Constance Mellon's 'Library Anxiety': An Appreciation and a Critique." *College & Research Libraries* 76, no. 3: 268–75. doi:10.5860/crl.76.3.268.

Harper, K., S. Hutton, C. Will, and S. Welch. 2016. "Library Transformations: Students as Participatory Design Ethnographers" (Introduction to the special issue). *AnthroZine* September: 8–11.

Jennings, K.A. 1993. "Recruiting New Populations to the Library Profession." *Journal of Library Administration* 19: 175–91.

Jiao, Q.G., A.J. Onwuegbuzie, and S.L. Bostick. 2004. "Racial Differences in Library Anxiety among Graduate Students." *Library Review* 53, no. 4: 228–35. doi:10.1108/00242530410531857.

Jones, S.D., and B. Murphy. 2019. *Diversity and Inclusion in Libraries: A Call to Action and Strategies for Success.* Lanham: Rowman & Littlefield.

Katapol, P. 2010. "Information Anxiety, Information Behavior, and Minority Graduate Students." *Proceedings of the American Society for Information Science and Technology,* February 3,

Lanclos, D. 2016. "Ethnographic Approaches to the Practices of Scholarly Communication: Tackling the Mess of Academia." *Insights* 29: 239–48.

Lanclos, D.A., and A. Asher. 2016. "'Ethnographish': The State of the Ethnography in Libraries." *Weave: Journal of Library User Experience* 1, no. 5.

Lewis, D.W. 2016. *Reimagining the Academic Library.* Lanham: Rowman & Littlefield.

Lockton, D., D. Harrison, and N.A. Stanton. 2010. "The Design with Intent Method: A Design Tool for Influencing User Behaviour." *Applied Ergonomics* 41, no. 3: 382–92.

Ryan, G.W., and H.R. Bernard. 2003. "Techniques to Identify Themes." *Field Methods* 15, no. 1: 85–109.

Tunstall, E.D. 2013. "Decolonizing Design Innovation: Design Anthropology, Critical Anthropology and Indigenous Knowledge." In *Design Anthropology: Theory and Practice,* ed. Wendy Gunn, Ton Otto, and Rachel Charlotte Smith, 232–50. London: Bloomsbury.

University of Massachusetts Amherst. 2017. *Campus Climate Survey: Abridged Report.*

US Department of Education. 2017. *Status and Trends in the Education of Racial and Ethnic Groups 2017.* National Center for Education Statistics.

CHAPTER TEN

Extravagance Outside of Anthropology: How to Sell Analytic Induction to Entrepreneurs

James Mullooly

The core competency of anthropological field research is analytic induction, a skill that has uncanny similarities to entrepreneurs' natural gift for "thinking out of the box."

This is the first line of the "pitch" I make to approximately 150 business students each semester in an introductory entrepreneurship class at a large public university in central California. As a guest speaker from the Department of Anthropology, I start by pointing out the similarities between anthropology and entrepreneurship. Traditionally, entrepreneurs were natural innovators who had an intuitive knack for bringing new things to the world. Now that business schools are teaching this, I point out that anthropology has been formally training students to do this sort of out-of-the-box thinking for about a century.

A number of years ago, I was awarded a grant to design and teach a course that would extend entrepreneurship across the curriculum of my university. The class, Applied Anthropology of Entrepreneurship, was successful, which led to further developments with colleagues in the colleges of Business and Engineering. Additionally, the program asked me to become a guest lecturer in its main introductory class so that I could both illustrate who I am as a member of their faculty and what anthropology has to offer business majors focused on entrepreneurship. My participation in this program and my visits to the introductory section have grown into a multi-class set of lectures where I assign one of the major assignments for the class, grade it, and return to talk about what they learned.

After years of trial and error, I believe I've come up with an effective means of catching the attention of these innovators-in-training for a long enough period to enable them to find some anthropology that is cool enough to be useful to them. Convincing them of this starts with extravagant ignorance.

EXTRA-VAGANCE AND IGNORANCE

Selling anything to salespeople is challenging, particularly when the buyers (business majors) typically know more about selling than the seller (anthropology professor), so my attempts to "add value" – or what we call "appear cool," disruptive, or useful – for these students have been a major part of my preparation for these lectures. Adding to this challenge is the complexity of the subject matter I refer to as "analytic induction." Analytic induction refers to the logical process that enables a participant observer to follow a hunch through the unraveling of complex cultural phenomena into a relatable story. Whereas "inspirational induction" can be thought of as unexpected "ah ha" moments of epiphany, analytic induction implies efforts that intentionally lead to such clarity. I humbly put forth that I know the material as well as anyone could, having written and taught about it for so many years. Additionally, I can attest, as authoritatively as I am able, that this observational technique will make these students better innovators.

But knowing something and being able to bring another to that knowing is often the crux of the problem. It is a problem for those who sell as well as for those who teach. After many attempts at improving this teaching, I have opted to go over the top. Rather than being more restrained in my efforts to reach across disciplinary boundaries, my solution was extravagance and, when that was not enough, I strived for extravagant extravagance or, as Henry David Thoreau put it, "Extra-vagance"! My use of Thoreau's coinage came from Boon's brilliant use of it (1999). Extra-vagance refers to acts of excessive elaborateness that are the norm throughout human ritual but which are rarely noticed without explicit attention. Additionally, explicit attention to such acts can help confront traditional biases.

Extra-vagance is a reminder that complexity need not be forgotten while popularizing a topic.

Rather than convincing them that I knew anything about business, my approach was to observe that I knew almost nothing about it. And that there is far more that I do not know than what I know. I then extend this metaphor to observe that this is the case for all of us and that any value I might have as an instructor would be to help them focus on their ignorance. Scroggins (2017) effectively contextualizes the theoretical lineage of ignorance as a philosophy of education within anthropology of education and as opposed to other uses of this conceptualization.

Successful students often attempt to outsmart each other with bigger and brighter illustrations of their mastery because schooling rewards knowledge performance. But knowledge production moves toward what we do not know. If you ask a successful scientist what they are interested in, they describe what they have yet to discover.

Knowledge production moves toward what we do not know. If you ask a successful scientist what they are interested in, they describe what they have yet to discover.

Firestein (2012) discusses the hitherto unknown unnoticed importance of ignorance in the process of how scientists actually function in direct opposition to how science is taught. Higher education struggles with this irony. But I am getting ahead of myself. I will now explain how I am making anthropology a little cooler.

THE ROAD TO COOL

My original doctoral training in applied anthropology at Teachers College, Columbia University, introduced me to a holistic perspective that granted no primary authority to any particular view. Like me, most of the students in the program were professionals who had already proven themselves in other areas prior to starting doctoral work in anthropology. This milieu was the arena of a perpetual struggle for attention by equally matched forces of authority and utility (see Figure 10.1).

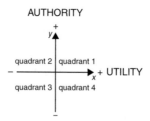

Figure 10.1. The authority-utility problem.

The program continually pushed us past a simplistic, single dichotomy of impractical authoritative knowledge on one end and useful but untested knowledge on the other. Rather than granting all the rewards to the most authoritative or the most useful with a single blunt measuring stick, the blurring of practicality and scholarly legitimacy were comfortable dancing partners. This training helped me reach beyond my department and college when I became a professor. As a junior faculty member, I spent much of my time away from anthropology and strived to get involved with colleagues across campus.

Specifically, I applied for a grant on my campus that attempted to expand entrepreneurship education outside of the College of Business. Being awarded this grant led to a number of other opportunities. This ended up aligning perfectly with my growth as an applied anthropologist at a higher educational institution who has spent his career attempting to practice anthropology outside of anthropology. As a result of receiving this grant, I was invited to other professional organizations dominated by people from business. The same tensions that I found in my doctoral program between "authors" and "practitioners" I found at these conferences between professors of business and successful business people without advanced degrees.

Outside of anthropology, the USASBE (United States Association for Small Business and Entrepreneurship) and programs launched and supported by the Coleman Foundation and the Kauffman Foundation were great networking and professional development opportunities for me and my colleagues. For example, I was awarded scholarships to attend USASBE's Experiential Classroom conference, a three-day clinic at the University of Florida for faculty new to teaching entrepreneurship. This helped me build a course in applied anthropology of entrepreneurship that I taught for a number of years to both social science and business majors. I also participated in the development of a VentureWell grant with other members of my campus to launch a three-college initiative where students from engineering, entrepreneurship, and anthropology worked in teams to develop a market-worthy product as their senior project. This initiative produced some immediate fruit in the form of conference awards for best papers, but after a few years, the program was dismantled due to competing programmatic requirements between the colleges.

The Participatory Design Conference was another very influential opportunity for the sort of synthetic thinking and bridge building required in this sort of work. This biannual conference brings together a host of practitioner-scholars from a wide variety of fields whose work relies upon design in some way.

Within anthropology, NAPA (the National Association for the Practice of Anthropology) and EPIC (the Ethnographic Praxis in Industry Conference) made all of these opportunities possible for me. All of the first connections I made to these other organizations started here. NAPA hosts events every year at the national AAA (American Anthropological Association) conference, and EPIC, like the Participatory Design Conference, is a venue that is very diverse in its membership.

TINKERING AND SHOWMANSHIP

My most effective approach to bring anthropology outside of the discipline is formal instruction, in the classical sense, but within that, it involves a fair amount of tinkering and showmanship. How to most effectively bring "out-of-the-box thinkers" out of their box is a perpetual struggle but the ignorance angle is one of the more powerful means I have found to do this. Rather than impress an audience with how much I know, I entice them with the wonder of all of the unknown unknowns. Ignorance seems to have as much impact as the classical exotic material for which anthropologists are notorious. For example, when I ask the class about one of the most impactful innovations of our species, students never suggest sewing needles, but there is no denying the radical power that warmer clothes had for Neolithic hunter-gatherers' survival! Although that is a popular part of my presentation, a later slide depicting the observation that the vast majority of our universe is composed of dark, "mysterious" matter always seems to make them pause in wonder for longer.

Within the academy, support has come more in the form of a slow and gradual respect for these skills than through one main event. Earning credibility at a university takes time, and earning it outside of one's home college of social sciences takes more time. So, in addition to attending anthropology conferences, I have attended business and specifically entrepreneurship conferences, as mentioned. Happily, I have found that the more applied the conference, the more funding there is often to be found to attend. Beyond this, some business faculty and full-time entrepreneurs are reluctant to listen to an academic who has never run his own business, preferring the relative safety of their side of the theory-practice tension divide.

Although crossing this divide is typically impossible, there was one moment where my credibility among the target audience of entrepreneurs hit a high point. While I was presenting a paper at a business conference, the very successful founder of a well-known Fortune 500 company publicly agreed with me that indeed entrepreneurs and anthropologists do seem to think and see the world in similar ways. During my presentation, I displayed a PowerPoint slide that included a table (see Table 10.1) comparing entrepreneurs to anthropological participant observers. I was emphasizing that the "out-of-the-box" thinking with which many successful entrepreneurs are born is something anthropologists are trained to do. I made this observation about 10 years ago, when it was fashionable to ask the question, "are entrepreneurs born or made?" At that time, published articles on the entrepreneur ontogeny had waxed in scholarly business journals. Now that many university-based programs in entrepreneurship are formally established, the need for this debate has waned.

In the broadest sense, my audience includes anyone unaware of the practical value of naturalistic observation. More narrowly, I have spent over a decade enticing entrepreneurs and entrepreneurs-in-training to become more empirical and rigorous in their consideration of potential opportunities based on exercises intended to make them better observers of mundane behavior and more reflective about the implications of these behaviors.

Table 10.1. Similarities between entrepreneurs and anthropologists.

Entrepreneurs by nature	Anthropologists by training	Application
See the big picture	Think holistically	Visionary, iconoclastic
Forward looking	Evolutionary approach	Predict future demands
Understand consumers	Insider/outsider perspectives	Predict market value
Think outside the box	Analytic induction	Keen observers, see opportunities

Cool is about popularizing these ideas while extravagance ensures that the complex profundity of these ideas is not reduced to simplified slogans. For the editors of this work, "cool" does not imply reductive or simplistic. Cool is awe inspiring and engaging at a glance. An extra-vagant look at induction was how I attempted to make anthropology cool enough for non-anthropologists to readily recognize its usefulness.

"Cool" does not imply reductive or simplistic. Cool is awe inspiring and engaging at a glance. An extravagant look at induction was how I attempted to make anthropology cool enough for non-anthropologists to readily recognize its usefulness.

THE LECTURE

On the first day, I give a lecture, which starts with a variety of illustrations of the unexpected value of ignorance. After many years of trying to use examples from anthropology, business, philosophy, and astrophysics, my most successful means of getting my point across has been through classic storytelling. Now, I start with the story of Pandora's Box.

The story begins with Zeus's anger at Prometheus (Greek for "forethought") for stealing fire from the gods to help humanity. To curse Prometheus and humanity, the gods create the beautiful Pandora and the horrible box. But after being offered the beguiling Pandora, Prometheus ignores the data before his eyes (the lovely Pandora) and, following a hunch, refuses the gift. Prometheus's brother, Epimetheus (Greek for "afterthought"), accepts the gift and as a result curses humanity to eternal suffering after Pandora opens the forbidden box of trouble.

Figure 10.2. The induction/deduction cycle.

I then explain that the titans represent two important methods of reasoning (Promethean induction and Epimethean deduction) and that these two approaches to making sense of the world are not in opposition to each other but are in fact complementary. Similar to the dualistic cosmology of Chinese philosophy described as yin and yang, both are required to reason.

Of the many definitions of induction and deduction I've used, the one that is most relatable can be depicted as a circular track with curated knowledge on top and raw data on the bottom. Whereas the Promethean analyst (e.g., anthropologists and entrepreneurs) will start at the bottom of the circle and work their way around and around from there, the Epimethean analyst (e.g., statisticians and chemists) starts at the top.

THE ASSIGNMENT

Following these illustrations, I get right down to the details of the point-bearing assignment, which aligns with a technical skill in business referred to as "opportunity analysis." I call the task ethnographic opportunity analysis and ask that students observe an existing service/product with the intention of looking for opportunities to improve or "add value" to that experience. Students must find a routine, taken-for-granted task/service/product and then "thickly describe" it – that is, empirically describe what they observed. Then, in a two-page "pitch," they are required to share their observations and suggest how they could improve the task/service/product. My hope was to get students to deeply observe routine behavior and, from that, begin to understand their customers better. I included a variety of details and a grading rubric to illustrate all of this in greater detail.

THE WORKAROUND WORKAROUND

After teaching in this manner for about five years, I noticed that about half of each class seemed to understand the exercise and produce work illustrating some level of what I'm calling analytic induction (in the voice of business students, "thinking outside of the box" as evidenced in one's observational and reasoning skills). Most of the other half of the students wrote reports that receive satisfactory grades due to matters of form and diligence, but they miss the mark in terms of effectively illustrating evidence of thick description and inductive analysis.

Business students are clever, and entrepreneurial thinkers are always thinking up new ideas. Normally beneficial, these habits can sometimes get in the way of scientific rigor. There are two primary distractions to students' understanding: "pet projects" and "a results orientation." The solution to this challenge has been to emphasize that rather than looking for how consumers *could* use a *new* service/product, the goal is to observe how consumers actually *do* use an *existing* service/product with the intention of looking for opportunities to improve or "add value" to that experience.

The "hung up on results" group tension is by far the largest impediment to moving business students and entrepreneurs past their own great ideas and into actually getting out of their heads and into the empirical realities beyond their own cleverness.

The only way I found to prevent students from thinking about solutions to problems was to ask them to no longer think them up. The efforts disrupt the pet-project focus, which takes much more effort. My solution is the workaround. For years, I was frustrated at the repeated habits that the students would fall into in terms

The "hung up on results" group tension is by far the largest impediment to moving business students and entrepreneurs past their own great ideas and into actually getting out of their heads and into the empirical realities beyond their own cleverness.

of focusing on their pet projects, seemingly unable to see anything but their own ideas.

I was thinking about how I could interrupt these students' implicit preferences for their own ideas when it dawned on me that inviting them to limit their scope to hacks might work. As a result, one semester, I described the essence of the project as a search for ways to add value, but I limited them to solutions that they had actually observed – that is, I very intentionally removed the "think up solutions" feature in this assignment. Rather, I requested that students observe other people solving problems in a rather mundane, unplanned, off-the-cuff manner.

Classic illustrations of this can be seen in ethnography and design projects where the observer notices the subject doing something out of the ordinary, like pulling pants inside out before they put them in the washing machine (i.e., the classic workaround to avoid color fading). In the hands of detergent merchants, awareness of this workaround is as much a potential gold mine as it was for Proctor & Gamble. The story behind Go-Gurt is another illustration of observers noting parents' attempted workarounds in trying to provide healthy snacks for their kids while out on the town and the solution that food processors can think up in response to these observations.

Buddhist master Shunryu Suzuki once taught that "[i]n a fog, you do not know you are getting wet, but as you keep walking you get wet little by little." Fog can get one just as wet as a torrential downpour, but noticing this may require a new perspective. My success in this work relies more on my willingness to help a colleague teach his class than fulfilling my personal mission to evangelize anthropology across the academy.

I started this project with the hope of turning business majors into anthropologists. Instead, I have helped my business college improve their program and make future business graduates better at the work they do through increased awareness of how humans behave. My core challenge was to help students better observe routine behavior. It is easy to observe something very strange but it is hard to observe something that is a mundane part of one's life. Simply asking students to do this failed, and it failed with an ever-increasing list of constraining requirements applied year after year. If I had an entire semester with these students, it might have been possible, but in a shorter time frame, it was not. Once I shifted this project to a task where students had to look for something specific (a workaround), it became much easier for non-anthropology students to conduct this observation successfully. Although I still strive to get students to be more mindful in terms of their observational awareness, it is frankly much easier to ask them to look for something specific. In doing so, they trick themselves into attending to mundane details. And through that process, they begin to build a deeper understanding of their clients and humanity.

FOR DISCUSSION

1 The excessively elaborate approach the author used to instruct his students helped them move from a comfortable knowledge space to an uncomfortable ignorance space in an effort to get them thinking inductively. How else might extra-vagance be invoked in an effort to improve instruction or analysis?

2 Using ignorance rather than knowledge as the primary organizing principle behind the author's presentation was an effective means of engaging a new audience. What are the opportunities and limitations to this instructional approach?

3 The authority-utility problem (where academic institutional authority ignores useful solutions generated in industry) might never go away, but it needs to be perpetually critiqued. How can practitioners become more relevant to academic knowledge production and vice versa? What could be the ways forward for coproduction of knowledge?

4 The noted similarities between entrepreneurs and anthropologists could become the locus of further fruitful innovations in business or qualitative methodology. How might the naturally inductive, out-of-the-box thinking of entrepreneurs better inform ethnography, one of the few truly inductive practices in the sciences?

5 Asking people to limit their observations to workarounds and not get "hung up on results" was a very productive solution to the author's challenge of helping students move past their own common sense. How could this technique be deployed to assist in the production of empirical observations outside of the classroom?

REFERENCES

Boon, J. 1999. *Verging on Extravagance Anthropology, History, Religion, Literature, Arts ... Showbiz.* Princeton: Princeton University Press.

Firestein, S. 2012. *Ignorance: How It Drives Science.* New York: Oxford University Press.

Scroggins, M. 2017. "Ignoring Ignorance: Notes on Pedagogical Relationships in Citizen Science." *Engaging Science, Technology, and Society* 3: 206–23. https://doi.org/10.17351/ests2017.54.

PART FOUR

Creatives

CHAPTER ELEVEN

Rez-Colored Glasses: Disentangling Indigenous Lives from the Colonial Gaze

Gregg Deal and Kerry Hawk Lessard

People don't really like Indians.... Oh, they like their own conceptions of the Indian – usually the Plains Indian, romantic and noble and handsome....

But Indians in America ... have really been viewed as something other than human beings by the larger society. The Indian of reality is a paradox – a monster to himself and a non-person to society.

Fritz Scholder (1937–2005)

BEING INDIGENOUS IN AMERICA

Being Indigenous in America is an odd sort of thing. Everyone has an opinion on who you are and who you are supposed to be while the opinion that counts the least is your own. You must exist in defiance of the tropes and stereotypes you've had no role in creating, but because they titillate the settler gaze, they become the defining vision of what you should look like, how you should speak, and even what your name is.

Take, for instance, Gregg Deal's performance art piece, "The Last American Indian on Earth," a work that explores the (mostly) inept relationship between Americans and American Indians. Wearing Plains-style regalia – think headdress, breechclout[1] and beaded moccasins – Gregg went about mundane routines in public places, interacting with, well, the general public (see Figure 11.1). The idea was to see how folks would behave, what they might say, and to document every cringeworthy moment.

It was during an in-character stroll on the National Mall in Washington, DC, that Gregg was approached by a woman demanding to know his tribal affiliation. In this interaction, she proclaims herself "part Cherokee" and indignantly tells him that *she* doesn't go walking around "looking like that." It's only when Gregg identifies himself as a citizen of the Pyramid Lake Paiute that her outrage turns to adoration and, more intriguing, her statements go from emic to etic. Clutching Gregg's arm, cooing and snuggling, this erstwhile gatekeeper of Indigenous identity declares it the happiest day of her life to meet a "real Indian." And faster than you can say, "Wilma Mankiller," she is drinking from the trough of romanticism to the point of intoxication.

But that's not the end. The denouement of this exchange is her question, "What's your name?" When the answer is "Gregg" – the actual Indigenous person's name – the truth is met with disappointment. "Gregg" somehow lacks the exoticism that an "Indian name" should have. This doesn't satisfy the colonial desire and Gregg is repeatedly cajoled to share his "real name" – the name that will live up to the fantasy of who and what an Indigenous person should be. Finally, Gregg relents, offering up the name Walking Eagle … which is, of course, an old Charlie Hill gag. You see, an eagle only walks when it's too full of shit to fly.

So, those whose views of Native lives are based on cartoons, Kevin Costner, and old westerns – that's our "public." And it is our intention to shake that public from its fever dream of ripped warriors and submissive butter maidens, insisting instead that they listen to Indigenous people telling our own stories in our own voices.

---

1 To prove a point, when trying to decide if we wanted to use "breechclout" or "breechcloth," we consulted Google. The first ad? "5 PC Cherokee Warrior Costume" from a site called Spicy Lingerie. Go ahead. Try it for yourself.

Figure 11.1. "The Last American Indian on Earth."

ANTHROPOLOGY, MEET ART

Apart from its *naissance* as a colonial enterprise, there's much to recommend the science of anthropology. Think of almost any slice of human behavior, whether the cattle herding of the Nuer or condom negotiation practices in sex work, and anthropology works it like a Rubik's cube. But whereas anthropology itself is as interesting as cultural practices are wide, how about anthropological writing? Not so much. It's often too dense, too jargonized, and, ironically, so obfuscatory that it's hard to engage. In short, it loses its cool.

And that's precisely the dichotomy Kerry wrestled with. Growing up separated by the Carlisle Indian Boarding School, the sense of personal displacement is profound. Being the descendant of a boarding school survivor first, and a medical anthropologist second, Kerry sought to untangle the impacts of *historical trauma,* a term that refers to the cumulative effects of "emotional and psychological wounding over the lifespan and across generations, emanating from massive group trauma" on the lives of contemporary Native people. And while believing the theoretical lens through which we might view these experiences is transformative and healing, Kerry acknowledged that her research and writing on the subject would have a limited audience. It would likely never reach the people who might benefit most: members of the urban Indian community in which she lives. There had to be a better way.

Enter Gregg Deal. As a visual and performance artist living in the DC area, Gregg's work – like "The Last American Indian on Earth" and "Missing Indian Wall" – unpacked the way Native people are perceived and the ways in which these (mis)perceptions fuel racism, oppression, and inequity. This was deeply personal for Gregg, himself a tribal citizen, the descendant of boarding school survivors, and the father of Native children who will live in a world that refuses to see them for who they are.

We were both involved in local activism to force change to the name of the DC NFL franchise, but it wasn't until we were locked in heated debate about Aaron Huey's rez poverty porn that we realized the potential of marrying our skill sets. After all, we were concerned with the same things – the constraints we felt imposed upon us, the injustice facing our relatives, and the horrifying things non-Natives would say within earshot – but approached them in different ways. Yet the more we talked, the more apparent it became that the anthropological theories and concepts Kerry wrote about were perfectly conceptualized in Gregg's art.

Our first collaboration, "Redskin," was a pop-up solo exhibition during Art All Night: Nuit Blanche, the annual Washington, DC, overnight arts festival. This multimedia event was anchored by a performance art piece in which several "antagonists" hurled invective at Gregg, who sat there and took it, never saying a word in response or defense (Figure 11.2). Kerry culled parts of this "script" directly from comments on *Washington Post* articles challenging the name of Dan Snyder's football team. Comments like, "Just remember you lost the war and should be greatful [sic] you have a place to live." While it's often said that people would never say in person the things they write in online anonymity, the reality is that these comments reflect the dehumanization of

Figure 11.2. "Redskin."

Indigenous people emboldened by the cartoonish ways we have been portrayed since the boats arrived. Gregg's performance, then, becomes the embodiment of what hateful words would look like if they were people as well as what it's like to nurture Indigenous selfhood while navigating settler colonialism.

In a nutshell, this is how we work: we observe the ways non-Natives construct a version of Indigeneity that is at turns romanticized, debasing, piteous, sexualized, and quite often, all of the above. We then deconstruct that image by engaging decolonized viewing and reframing the interaction from an overtly Indigenist perspective. In our partnership, Gregg creates visual and performance art that satirizes stereotypes and reclaims the Indigenous image while Kerry supports that art with anthropological research, Indigenous scholarship, and traditional knowledge. And though the order of that work may change, we create serious and intelligent art that opposes the insensitive, uninformed, appropriative, unjust, and plain wrong ideas non-Natives have about what it means to be Indigenous.

CREATING OUR AUDIENCE

Since his 2005 work with late Luiseño artist James Luna, Gregg has steadily built a body of provocative art and an impressive internet following. Thanks to an epic marketing blunder by clothing retailer Gap in 2012, Gregg's response to their MANIFEST DESTINY T-shirt went viral. With mock-ups that read FORCED ASSIMILATION and MASS GENOCIDE, he garnered international attention when flipping the colonial script. Followed by appearances on *Totally Biased with W. Kamau Bell* and *The Daily Show* with Jon Stewart, Gregg's profile as an artist/activist afforded a certain level of built-in support. This isn't to say that it has been (or is) easy, but visibility helps.

Remember the 1990s, when Jessica Seinfeld was sneaking spinach and carrots into brownies to make them healthier? Well, we've been able to sneak solid anthropological ideas into street art. Sometimes it's not even so sneaky, like the 2016 "Ethnographic Zoo," performed at the Denver Art Museum during the time of Gregg's Native arts residency.

Remember the 1990s, when Jessica Seinfeld was sneaking spinach and carrots into brownies to make them healthier? Well, we've been able to sneak solid anthropological ideas into street art.

Conceived to deconstruct the commodification and consumption of the Indigenous image, the title explicitly refers to Vine Deloria Jr.'s *Custer Died for Your Sins* (1969). In response to the question of why Native people should be the "private zoos for anthropologists," Gregg once again made the word flesh, dusting off the bonnet and Pendleton blanket and sitting down behind a stanchion rope (Figure 11.3). The sign outside? "Do Not Feed The Stereotype."

On the other hand – and we know this will come as a shock – anthropology can take itself too seriously. That's why our partnership works both ways.

While we are using Gregg's art as a vehicle for theory, we're also using that theory as a way to bring Indigenous voices and critique into the academy. Considering how often Native cultures are the subject of study but Native people have been historically excluded, that's no small thing.

While we are using Gregg's art as a vehicle for theory, we're also using that theory as a way to bring Indigenous voices and critique into the academy. Considering how often Native cultures are the subject of study but Native people have been historically excluded, that's no small thing.

Figure 11.3. "Ethnographic Zoo."

And also changing, thank goodness! We wonder, though, if Ella Cara Deloria, a Dakota ethnographer whose work was arguably exploited by Franz Boas (see Lewis 2001) could ever have imagined Indian people at the lectern taking the discipline to task for its bad behavior. Then again, maybe that's why her nephew Vine seemed to target anthropology with such glee. Anyway, the point is that working in an interdisciplinary collaboration has, for us, afforded the support that either one of us individually may not have enjoyed.

As we mentioned, Gregg's social media profile and our shared activist street cred allowed us access to certain spaces and audiences where we could have the kinds of conversations we wanted to start ... and sometimes force. Again, it won't necessarily work this way for everyone (or for us, every time), but our insistence on visibility opened doors.

In 2015, for example, Woolly Mammoth Theatre Company in Washington, DC, extended the invitation for us to do a Q&A after a performance of Gregg's "Pan Indian Romantic Comedy." While this provided Gregg and Kerry a forum to discuss his artwork and unpack the anthropological content within, it also gave us access to an audience that was not necessarily receptive to what we were putting down. A memorable moment during the Q&A came when a man, legs crossed, leaning back with arms draped across two adjacent seats, asked, "Why don't you just get over it?" It was as if one of the online commenters stepped out from behind the screen to exert his white privilege. In return, we asked the questioner if he would pose that same question to Elie Wiesel or to any Holocaust survivor. This man was simply unable to relate to the fact that what happened to our people was nothing less than genocide or that our concerns could possibly be more important than his love for his team and the right to wear a dismembered head on his belt buckle.

Certainly, other audiences – perhaps even most audiences – were interested in what we had to say, but it has been our experience that we can expect pushback when we, as Indian people, don't conform to the stereotype people hold in their heads. It's as if we are being unspeakably impolite when we dare speak for ourselves. Or have blue eyes. Or a name that's not "Rainbow Wolf." As Gregg once observed, "American culture doesn't say, 'Hey, there's a sovereign group of people over here, we should hold them up and help them carry themselves.' Instead, it's 'Hey look, these people over here are suffering, and we're going to tell their story for them.'" That's one of the challenges we face. And of course, not the only one.

WHOSE STORY?

Gregg is known to quote Dave Skylark's infamous line from *The Interview* (2014), "They hate us 'cause they AIN'T us!" Joking aside, anthropology, for all of its pretense of wokeness, has a real problem with ownership. Specifically, anthropology – and anthropologists – tend to exert a kind of authority over the stories, practices, and identities of the Native people with whom they come in contact. Kerry recalls a particularly distasteful conversation with a professor of cultural anthropology talking about work she did with "her" Indians. Anthropologists often make us in the image *they* are comfortable with rather than allowing us to exist as we actually are.

In trying to advance our work, it's been very important that we privilege the work of other Indigenous scholars and that we honor

Indigenous ways of knowing and sharing information. It seems, though, that the academy just isn't ready for that. In fact, at one point, we were invited to contribute our work to an anthology. We were intentional about using storytelling to discuss the importance of place-based relationships to our understanding of being Indigenous people. Ironically, the same academy that sought our participation (to write about the Indigenous experience) found our way of doing so (using traditional practices of information sharing) "off-putting."

Inevitably, an ongoing challenge remains the perhaps unconscious tendency of a majority non-Native public to view Indigenous people as somehow less than capable of exercising our own agency, controlling our own science, and holding an unflattering mirror to settler colonialism. It would almost seem that Fritz Scholder, with whose words we began this chapter, might really have been on to something.

In the sense that engaging with cool anthropology – that is, unconventional ways of disseminating credible anthropological content – allowed us multiple opportunities to present a more authentically Indigenous narrative, we were able to experiment with art and anthropology working as one brain.

While Gregg's work stands on its own, there have been some concepts – like that of the ethnographic zoo or the way mascots trigger historical trauma – that when informed by anthropological thinking, allow for a more nuanced interrogation of creative ideas. In our partnership, Kerry has chosen to play a role that works more in service to the art itself. This is in keeping with the original premise that Gregg's art is more accessible to those who might not otherwise engage with anthropology through journals or monographs or conference attendance. Yawn.

More importantly, elevating art resonates within Indian Country, which is as it should be given the damaging role anthropology has played historically.

From a larger perspective, we believe that such collaborative efforts reaffirm the need for Indigenous artists and scientists to be fully in control of our own work, our own words, our own worlds. Only by insistently and unapologetically asserting our right to occupy these spaces will we unseat the dominant colonial narratives and reclaim our rightful voice.

Elevating art resonates within Indian Country, which is as it should be given the damaging role anthropology has played historically.

For us, the opportunity to participate in cool anthropology projects provides an alternate framework for sharing the ideas that we feel are essential to the visibility and equity we seek. Why is that important? Because for every person who tells us that we should have bigger things to worry about than mascots or Halloween costumes, we have a body of work to dismiss that red herring. What we know – and what we can show through the use of visual and interactive art – is that these issues are absolutely interrelated.

When our people must navigate the misrepresentation and devaluation of our lands, cultures, and bodies daily, it sends an unmistakable message about our worth as human beings in the eyes of the society around us. And where these beliefs of depreciated self-worth gain traction, the more difficult it is to achieve the level of physical and emotional health that grows strong Native nations. The ability to create art and to tell stories, these were always medicine ways among our people. And though we make no claims to be medicine people, we do know that carrying on these traditions is of vast importance to our people. It is the legacy of our ancestors, and to them we owe an incredible debt. From them, we draw our resilience and in us lies the realization of their dream.

The ability to create art and to tell stories, these were always medicine ways among our people. And though we make no claims to be medicine people, we do know that carrying on these traditions is of vast importance to our people.

FOR DISCUSSION

1 Indigenous identity is too often framed by colonial assumptions and expectations rather than the lived reality of Indigenous people themselves. How can anthropologists address this historical framing in the context of their theoretical training?

2 Consider the ways that Indigenous people are expected to perform our cultures for the pleasure of colonial audiences and that boundaries on what is and is not for public consumption are not consistently respected. Consider the colonial sense of ownership of Indigenous

bodies and stories compared with Indigenous sover-
eignty and autonomy. Consider the implications this has
on the sense of identity and self-efficacy of Native people.
3 The anthropological toolkit can be used to empower
Native people to tell their own stories in ways that our
communities value, understand, and sustain. What are
the elements of the toolkit that could be most useful in
this pursuit and what does methods training look like in
this context?
4 Indigenous knowledge systems have been systematically
and violently dismantled. How can we affirm Indigenous
knowledge and knowledge production as inherently valuable and challenge Western hegemony? In other words,
why must we insist on forcing the round peg of Indigenous knowledge into the academy's square box?

REFERENCES

Deloria Jr., Vine. 1969. *Custer Died for Your Sins: An Indian Manifesto.* New York:
    Macmillan.
Lewis, Herbert S. 2001. "The Passion of Franz Boas." *American Anthropologist*
    103, no. 2: 447–67. https://doi.org/10.1525/aa.2001.103.2.447.
Rogen, Seth, and Evan Goldberg. 2014. *The Interview* [film]. Columbia
    Pictures.

CHAPTER TWELVE

Sonic Anthropology: From Remixing Archives to Reimagining Cultures

Tom Miller

This chapter looks back on three decades of sonic anthropology practice in three modes of research-based art: museum exhibitions, gallery installations, and radiophonics. Each of these projects involved remixing and reimagining archival ethnographic sound recordings for public presentation. Each can also be considered an experiment in ethnographic conceptualism as defined by Nikolai Ssorin-Chaikov (2013, 5–6):

1 Ethnographic conceptualism posits a symmetry of art and anthropology.
2 Ethnographic conceptualism is conceptual art conducted as ethnography.
3 Ethnographic conceptualism is ethnography conducted as conceptual art.

In their various ways of working with recorded sound archives, these case studies are also in agreement with a fourth principle stated by Ssorin-Chaikov:

4 In contrast to ethnography as participant observation of what exists, ethnographic conceptualism explicitly constructs the reality that it studies.

MUSEUM PROJECTS

Museum anthropology became more formally established as a subdiscipline of anthropology during the 1990s, a period when old colonialist frames were being reexamined and recast into more reflexive, self-conscious models of collecting and display. As a senior scientific assistant and guest curator at the American Museum of Natural History, I was enmeshed in the history of anthropology, buried deep in vaults overflowing with iconic ethnographic collections. I absorbed a curatorial approach to juxtaposition and dialogue among objects of study as an organizing principle for research-based arts, whether working with artifacts, texts, sounds, or images.

Because of my background in ethnomusicology and theatrical sound design, American Museum of Natural History curator Enid Schildkrout asked me to create soundscape installations for "African Reflections: Art from Northeastern Zaire," a traveling exhibition that broke new ground in presenting art history in the context of science museums (Schildkrout and Keim 1990). The soundtracks accompanied objects and images from the American Museum's 1909–1915 Congo Expedition, including musical instruments and photo murals of a Mangbetu royal court orchestra (Miller 1992). We wove together audio sources, including Belgian colonial wax-cylinder field recordings, the renowned Hugh Tracey archive, and unused footage from the commissioned 1989 documentary film *Spirits of Defiance* by director Jeremy Marre. In a Museum for African Art symposium, "Africa by Design: Designing a Museum for the 21st Century," Schildkrout reflected on the sounds and images in the context of different overall exhibition environments and experiences:

> It's very interesting to contrast how "African Reflections" looked and felt at the American Museum of Natural History in New York, and how it felt at the National Museum of African Art in Washington, DC.... In New York it was a show about Africa, and in Washington it was a show about art objects....
>
> The difference was a couple of things. One was the way the space was arranged, and another was the use of photographs and sound. In Washington, they had eliminated three sound tapes we had strategically placed in the exhibition. In New York, we used

photographs as objects and as context, not specifically as information.... The feedback I've gotten from many people, and my own feeling, is that the exhibition didn't work as well in Washington ... it's not simply whether you use Plexi cases or you don't use Plexi cases, but how you think about space, and how you incorporate the Plexi and the other elements – color, visuals, sound – into the experience of the exhibition. (Roberts and Vogel 1994, 14–15)

"Drawing Shadows to Stone: Photographing North Pacific Peoples (1897–1902)" extended this role reversal, using artifacts to illustrate photographs rather than the other way around. This 1997–1998 exhibition, which I curated with Laurel Kendall and Barbara Mathé, marked the centennial of the American Museum of Natural History's landmark Jesup North Pacific Expedition – a massive collecting enterprise in northwestern North America and northeastern Asia organized by Franz Boas, founding father figure of American anthropology. Our journey from research to exhibition involved deep immersion in the voluminous archives of this most ambitious of collecting expeditions. To enhance the photographs and objects, I designed a multimedia "sound station" – state of the art for the 1990s – with producer Kevin Walker and sound mix by DJ Spooky. Visitors selected videos blending the earliest sound recordings from Siberia and northwestern North America with early and more recent photographs. Building on this curatorial approach, my subsequent doctoral dissertation fieldwork included distributing copies of archived shamans' songs from the Jesup collection to their originating communities in Siberia, Alaska, and British Columbia. This was a kind of ethnohistory in reverse: tracing sound objects from the museum archives back in time to their sources, interviewing contemporary people about them and virtually repatriating them to the descendants of the performers.

"Shamans of Siberia – Magicians, Mediums, Healers" was a 2008–2009 exhibition at the Linden State Museum of Ethnology in Stuttgart, Germany, one of Europe's oldest ethnographic museums. Organized in cooperation with the Russian Museum of Ethnography and curated by Erich Kasten, it was the largest and most comprehensive exhibition on the subject ever mounted in the West. My role as guest ethnomusicologist and media artist was to create an immersive space filling two large halls with sound, light, and images evoking the world of Siberian shamans.

Entitled *Schamanenreise* (Shaman's Journey), this installation formed a distinct aural and visual environment within the larger exhibition. A central goal was to inform the European audience about non-Western concepts of dealing with nature and the supernatural, to be treated in a respectful way. But how could we do justice to the phenomenon of shamanism from the point of view of the Indigenous people of Siberia, for whom it has been an important part of their collective identity? In the long wake of Soviet repression and social reorganization, they were still seeking new ways to reconnect to their own traditional worldviews. The overarching theme linking shamanic worldviews with traditional concepts of human relations with nature ran throughout the exhibition. We wanted to create an immersive environment, blending old and new media archives, to temporarily shift the museumgoer's mindset away from the evidence of objects and the analytic interpretation of words toward a more poetic, experiential receptivity to the power of sounds and images. We decided to break away from museological tradition by having no explanatory text at all in this section of the exhibition. Through video projections, special lighting, and 360-degree sound, visitors navigated a passage from the dawn chorus of birds and animals to the northern lights and the deep night chanting and drumming of shamanic ceremony. Century-old wax-cylinder recordings, contemporary field and studio recordings, and the sounds of shifting ice and Earth's magnetic field reverberated over 25 independently placed sound channels, creating an ever-shifting aural universe.

The shaman operates on worldly and otherworldly planes simultaneously, as both a skilled sender of spirit voices and a special listener who has the power to understand them. On one of the archival Jesup recordings, a Chukchi nonbinary shaman called Scratching Woman can be heard practicing a ghostly form of ventriloquism, skillfully throwing their voice and bouncing it off the reflecting walls of a small room until the spirits seemed to be coming from all directions. To reimagine this haunting effect, we used the visual programming language Max/MSP to mix the monaural 1901 wax-cylinder recording into eight channels of surround sound, whirling Scratching Woman's voice around listeners in imitation of this tour-de-force of spirit ventriloquism. (When these highly mobile sounds were first let loose in the historic building, the spooky vibrations resonated and traveled throughout the floors and walls, bringing staff members running to express concern for the well-being of the museum guards.) Another feature of our sound design was a series of long whispering tubes. Field recordings of shamanic chanting invoking spirits could be softly heard through them but only when the visitor stood in one spot, as if they were addressing each individual privately. The organizers hoped the overall experience of this exhibition might help lead people in the West (and perhaps even some in Russia) to reimagine cultures through these glimpses of hidden shamanic histories and to gain renewed confidence in these traditions amid the upheavals of a rapidly changing society.

GALLERY PROJECTS

"Secret Wars" was part of a yearlong installation series on the theme of battle held at the Proteus Gowanus interdisciplinary gallery in Brooklyn, New York. This project explored the cryptic ways of warfare waged behind the cloak of invisibility (see Leckert 2015, 158–61). As curators, Proteus Gowanus co-creative director Tammy Pittman and I invited artists from New York, Amsterdam, Berlin, and elsewhere to reveal gaps, silences, and blackouts that concealed vital and deadly knowledge. David Goren's "*Atencion! Seis Siete Tres Siete Cero*: The Mystery of the Shortwave Numbers Stations" was a room full of secrets where the shortwave radio signals of the mysterious "numbers stations" could be heard. These enigmatic transmissions, recitations of long streams of numbers punctuated by bursts of fragmentary speech, are believed to be encrypted messages meant for individual spies. When sunspots and atmospheric conditions are favorable, shortwaves can propagate and skip around the planet. The location of the receiver is unknown. The intended recipient decrypts the numbers using a one-time pad that they then destroy, rendering the code unbreakable. A private message sent through a public medium thus avoids detection by hiding in plain sight; the signal is potentially audible to anyone, but only one person understands its meaning. Inside the room, the hypnotically repetitive messages were beamed to gallery visitors who attempted to detect and decode the patterns and the meanings hidden in the continuous stream of cryptic voices.

The disappearing archive is a central figure for contemporary anthropology, as older collections built to preserve knowledge rapidly become obsolete artifacts of the vanishing analog era. The apparent rush to oblivion of rapidly degrading magnetic tapes and other physical recording media represents the specter of the twentieth century erasing itself. For the 2014 annual meeting of the American Anthropological Association, I was invited to be the guest curator, with Ethnographic Terminalia, of "The Bureau of Memories: Archives & Ephemera," an immersive installation in Washington, DC's Hierarchy gallery. This was one of a series of shows, distributed across a dozen North American cities from 2009 to 2019, in which the Ethnographic Terminalia (2014, 2015) curatorial collective pushed and expanded the boundaries of anthropological scholarship and contemporary art.

The rise of curatorial collectives, in parallel with the Occupy and Decolonize movements of the 2010s, is part of a wider decentering of institutional authority and control in the art and museum worlds. Anthropologists are developing experimental art-based methods of inquiry in research-based exhibitions as an alternative form of ethnographic practice and communication.

With "The Bureau of Memories" (see Figure 12.1), the Ethnographic Terminalia curatorial collective repositioned the archive as a waypoint in the production of ethnographic knowledge, contested histories, and shifting identities. Bringing out obscured traces of sounds, films, photographs, documents, and memories drawn from institutional and personal collections, participating anthropologists and artists created new works, remixing faded voices and ghostly moving images in a multisensory encounter with spectral presences from anthropology's past. The Bureau was an imaginary organization charged with a set of ambiguous and opaque functions related to history and memory, reassembling archival fragments in ways they were never intended to be.

To enter the space, visitors passed through Lina Dib's stairwell installation, where their movements triggered the familiar yet already half-forgotten sounds of such recently obsolete technology as dial-up modems and fax machines. Inside the gallery a "Schizophonic Archive" allowed visitors to call up old ethnographic field recordings on

Figure 12.1. "The Bureau of Memories." Photo: Tom Miller.

converted analog telephones. Further inside was a curated project space for installations, conversations, workshops, and presentations. The Bureau was structured through site-specific works, events organized by invited exhibitors, including John L. Jackson, Jr. and CAMRA (Collective for Advancing Multimodal Research Arts) from the University of Pennsylvania's Annenberg School of Communication, and an open call for submissions. The open call was a critical tool for supporting established and emerging artist-researchers, restaging elements from archival collections, and expanding the audience beyond the anthropology community. During its run as a pop-up installation, "The Bureau of Memories" attracted attention from the general public, the press, and the mayor's office as well as artists, archivists, and museum workers.

As curators, we sought artists and anthropologists working in the spaces between disciplinary boundaries to produce an exhibition that would resonate with the history and politics of the nation's capital. As the seat of both the federal government and the National Archives, the city of Washington is the symbolic center of American power and historical memory. Raul Ortega Ayala's piece "18 and a half minutes" actualized one of the most famous and consequential archival recordings in US history. At the heart of his documentary assemblage of audio, objects, and transcripts stood a 3D-printed rendering of a waveform: a spectrogram analysis of the notorious 18½-minute gap that led to the resignation of President Richard Nixon. In 1972, shortly after the Watergate break-in at the Democratic Party campaign headquarters, Nixon discussed the case with his chief of staff, H.R. Haldeman. Through a concealed switch installed in the Oval Office, Nixon secretly operated a tape recorder hidden in the White House floor. When the existence of the taping system was revealed and the Supreme Court forced the president to release the transcripts, there was a mysterious 18½-minute gap where the crucial incriminating conversation should have been. While the sounds and magnetic marks imprinted on the tape are consistent with a series of manual erasures, the words have never been recovered because of machine noise overwritten onto the erased portion. Ayala's precisely rendered object, a three-dimensional spectrogram of the gap, traced the exact microgeography of this secret aural history, including the erasures, machine noise, and the faint murmur of "ghost voices" in the bumps and grooves. The absence of the original content gives the famous gap its specific historical weight. While digital audio reconstruction has remained inconclusive, Ayala and "The Bureau of Memories" minded the gap by conjuring the spectral form of the cover-up into the daylight, converting invisible sonic history into a visible, tangible presence.

RADIOPHONIC PROJECTS

Another way of sounding out archives in "The Bureau of Memories" was realized in "Kabusha Radio Remix: Your Archive Questions Answered by Pioneering Zambian Talk Show Host, David Yumba (1923–1990)" by Debra Spitulnik Vidali and Kwame Phillips. Modeled after an African listening room of the 1980s, this installation reimagined taped broadcasts by using them to respond to present-day listeners. Vidali collected hours of tape of David Yumba, a famous Zambian radio host who died in 1990. He was better known as "Kabusha," after the name of his program, *Kabusha Takolelwe Bowa,* a Bemba proverb meaning "The Person Who Inquires First, Is Not Poisoned by a Mushroom." Listeners from all over Zambia used to write him letters asking for both personal and political advice, which he freely gave over the air. In the installation, which has since been shown at the British Museum, visitors were invited to write their own letters to Kabusha. Some of them were answered by the deconstructed and reassembled voice of Kabusha as remixed by Phillips. The recreated listening room experience incorporated the original flow of advertisements, music, and announcements, interwoven as if one was hearing an actual live broadcast commenting on current events.

Radio as a stage for political theater plays an especially important role in Africa, where a broadcast signal's ability to be present in both urban and rural areas forges community bonds as well as friction. In Zambia and Zimbabwe, the FM band is thriving, with national networks providing broad coverage and numerous small, independent community stations serving rural areas. In places with little or no internet access, the airwaves can be continuous and pervasive, like water flowing in a river.

In the late 1950s, the Tonga of British colonial Rhodesia and Northern Rhodesia (now the independent countries of Zimbabwe and Zambia, respectively) were divided, displaced, and dispossessed of their land on the shores of the Zambezi River by the construction of the Kariba Dam. This enormous hydroelectric power plant flooded the Zambezi Valley, creating the world's largest manufactured lake. While the dam has brought improvements to many people's lives, some Tonga groups resettled on arid land have struggled with periodic famine and drought. The two halves of the community have been separated by the vast Lake Kariba and the border between the two countries for the past 60 years. In 2018, community radio station Zongwe FM in Sinazongwe, Zambia, partnered with the Zubo Trust for women's development in Binga, Zimbabwe. They brought Tonga women from both sides of the lake together to raise awareness of social issues affecting women and girls, learn media production skills, make music together, and share their voices on the radio. Working with German radio artist and journalist Claudia Wegener (aka radio continental drift), they also launched *A*

Radio-Bridge across the Zambezi, a global collaboration inviting composers and radio artists around the world to freely remix recordings from the Zongwe FM–Zubo Trust broadcast archives. The resulting Bandcamp album, sold as an internet download to raise funds for the radio station and as a CD in the local marketplace to reach a greater Zambian audience, includes powerful tracks by L-ness (short for "Lioness"), aka Lydia Akwabi – one of Kenya's top hip-hop artists and a social scientist organizing poor women in Nairobi – and DJ Kwe, aka Crystal Favel, a Cree, Métis, and Irish sound artist from northwestern Canada. When it was my turn to contribute, I imagined a journey from the lowlands in the valley up to the high ground over the lake, where the signal carrying the Tongan women's voices can be heard loud and clear across the distance. Wegener describes the resulting remix as "layering the various vocal inputs from the Valley as they are representing multilayered resonating realities; perspectives on their home area are interacting with – and the ancient sounds of the Budima [funeral drums] are interweaving with – the young radio-makers' concerns."

In 2020, when the global coronavirus pandemic shut down university classes and forced people to stay home, anthropology students in my classes at Brooklyn College, City University of New York, listened to curated playlists from the archives of Zubo Trust and Zongwe FM; they then recorded audio letters in response, which we sent to their African counterparts. We received many voice messages in reply from students in Zambia and Zimbabwe expressing warm greetings, happiness, and heartfelt encouragement at the opening of this window of global communication in a difficult time of mutual isolation. An archived edited playlist, "Building Radio Bridges – Audio Letters between Lockdown NYC and the Zambezi Valley," is housed on the internet archive for anyone to listen to and remix, and an hourlong radio program based on the project is freely available from the archives of Wave Farm and WGXC community radio.

Located in New York State's Hudson Valley, Wave Farm is a nonprofit that successfully combines an innovative, genre-defining transmission arts program with WGXC FM, a highly engaged, independent community radio station run by local volunteers (see Joseph-Hunter 2011). For Wave Farm's *Short Waves/Long Distance* project, I created an imaginary audioscape, "Spectral Wars." This piece is an archival mix composed of shortwave interval signals – brief repeating fragments of

Figure 12.2. Zongwe FM. Photo: Claudia Wegener.

melody, speech, birds, animals, and other aural motifs broadcast at regular intervals to identify stations, mark program times, and hold down frequencies against potential rival broadcasters. In wars and conflict zones, interval signals can overtly carry symbolic political signals across national borders. At times, both official state-sponsored and clandestine rebel broadcasts can be captured among the waves of static drift. "Spectral Wars" reimagines spinning the dial and hearing signals from occupied territories and rebel camps through different regions and eras.

Some of the signals in the mix were broadcast from the wartime regimes and liberation fronts of past conflicts. On SoundCloud, the piece has drawn the heaviest traffic from the smallest countries in the mix. Because they are distant and few (though not "remote" – no one is marginal to themselves), search algorithms for these countries' names in metatags find fewer competing results and lead internet listeners in

Micronesia and Bhutan directly to the mix, where they can also find and follow each other's tracks.

Tuning the radio dial enacts a manual auditory mapping of imagined places onto invisible spaces. Moving beyond one-way broadcasting, radio in the twenty-first century is an interactive, multi-platform digital medium. Radio artists and radio activists are inventing new genres on- and offline. Online listening can be decoupled from synchronous time and reproduced on demand by individual listeners. On the internet, we can track and harvest data to learn more about listeners, but a certain randomness remains. A message beamed out in real time is received asynchronously by individuals scattered at an indeterminate number of geographic points, linked in an invisible temporary community.

Online listening can be decoupled from synchronous time and reproduced on demand by individual listeners.... A message beamed out in real time is received asynchronously by individuals scattered at an indeterminate number of geographic points, linked in an invisible temporary community.

Sound maps are another growing archival presence on the web. Stuart Fowkes's online project *Cities and Memory*, inspired by the magical realism of Italo Calvino's *Invisible Cities*, documents real sound worlds through field recordings ("City versions") alongside sound artists' imaginary sonic environments based on them ("Memory versions"). In 2016, *Cities and Memory* produced the first sound map of the London Underground, "The Next Station" (Bramley 2016). Coincidentally, it was also the centenary of World War I. As a contributor, I was given the contemporary sounds of the Angel underground railway station to remix and reimagine into a Memory version. The Angel station is located at the corner of Islington High Street, historically an important crossroads and a main transfer point for World War I troops heading to the battlefields of Europe. It was exactly 100 years since the 1916 Battle of the Somme, when more British soldiers were lost in a single day than on any other day in history. Reverberating like ghost voices in the remixed "Angels of Islington" are fragments of so-called descriptive sketches: contemporaneous reenactments recorded during the war and released to the wartime home-front public as popular audio dramas, from the excitement and goodbyes of leaving for the front to the poison gas bombardment and carnage of trench warfare from which tens of thousands never returned. In the reimagined Memory version, these voices echo and haunt the corridors of the busy tube station, mingling with the sounds of modern London.

After the 2015 vote on Brexit and the 2016 US election of Donald Trump, *Cities and Memory* contributors recorded and remixed the sounds of street demonstrations erupting all over the world for the *Protest and Politics* sound map project (Turk 2017). By this time, analog field recordings had become part of the historical past. For me it was a rather spooky experience of becoming an archaic exemplar emerging from the dusty archives, as Fowkes wrote:

> City version: The oldest recording in our Protest and Politics project, and one of the earliest recordings on Cities and Memory. Going back to January 1991, a protest in Washington DC against the first Gulf War, two days after the commencement of the US-led air war against Iraq, recorded by Tom Miller. It's a rare recording we're lucky to have, and it's interesting to look for similarities or differences in how we protest over a quarter of a century. Simon Woods brings the recording bang up to date, transforming it into a flashy news broadcast that's very much from 2017.

For his stirring Memory version, "Protest – A News Story," UK composer Simon Woods explained his process of reimagining my original field recording:

> The basic concept for the piece is the protest and the news reporting of the protest. The protest sounds make up the basic rhythm of the whole piece. The orchestra represents the news reporting. It takes the rhythm of the protest but tries to drown out the voices so they cannot be heard except on the news' terms. The protest voices do go away, but return later as protests do. The heroic trumpet represents the military who use emotion to quell protest – the patriotism argument. The drum machine rhythm is a nod to Paul Hardcastle's anti-war "19" – although the rhythm is quite different. It is the only electronic instrument in the piece. The pounding drums represent the war which is going on. I find it fascinating that a drum rhythm and voices/sounds playing in a protest in 1991 in Washington, USA can influence a piece of music composed in 2017 in the UK.

What are archival memories waiting for? Throughout the world, vast collections of sound recordings remain unheard and unknown. Recorded sounds of the past turn slowly into forgotten histories, waiting for a future resurfacing that might not ever come.

What are archival memories waiting for? Throughout the world, vast collections of sound recordings remain unheard and unknown. Recorded sounds of the past turn slowly into forgotten histories, waiting for a future resurfacing that might not ever come.

Archival recordings always contain the potential for a second life, to be heard anew and reimagined in the context of future recombinant soundscapes. Phonographic archives are a rich source for radiophonic reinvention and remix culture, linking ethnography, folklore, oral history, and archives with DJs, artists, activists, and communities. Sounding out silent voices, they are creating new genres in which to hear field recordings and listen to the past. In addition to research, exhibitions, performances, and transmission arts, they can be used for language education, fieldwork training, ethnographic study, and more. This type of reflexivity and creativity relies on information exchange, collaborative input, reimagination, and reinvention to produce experiences and knowledge beyond the restrictive category of "ethnographic" information. Linking the present with the past, repatriation with recombination and redistribution, from remix culture to reimagining cultures, sonic anthropology is both hyperlocal and transnational at the same time.

FOR DISCUSSION

1 A curatorial approach to art as anthropology and anthropology as art constructs new frameworks for presenting research. What makes something art?
2 Multisensory environments can deepen understanding by creating a bridge between evidence and experience. In which ways does experiential learning promote a deeper understanding of a particular topic?

3 Remixing archives reveals hidden meanings, conjuring the invisible out of the shadows and into an unknown presence. What sorts of opportunities are available to reconsider and potentially remix in your own work that might illuminate new insights?

4 Sonic anthropology provides a mobile, collaborative, and interactive medium for reimagining cultures. What is useful to communities about reimagining cultures in public spaces?

REFERENCES

Bramley, Ellie Violet. 2016. "Subterranean Sonic Blues? A Journey through the First Ever London Underground Sound Map." *The Guardian*, August 26.

Ethnographic Terminalia (Craig Campbell, Kate Hennessy, Fiona P. McDonald, Trudi Lynn Smith, Stephanie Takaragawa, Thomas Ross Miller). 2014. *The Bureau of Memories: Archives & Ephemera*. Washington, DC: American Anthropological Association.

Ethnographic Terminalia. 2015. "After the Bureau of Memories: Reflections at the Intersections of Archives, Art, and Anthropology." *Mnemoscape* 2.

Joseph-Hunter, Galen. 2011. *Transmission Arts: Artists & Airwaves*. New York: PAJ Publications.

Kasten, Erich, ed. 2021. *Schamanen Sibiriens und ihr Vermächtnis [Siberian Shamans and Their Legacy]*. Fürstenberg/Havel: Kulturstiftung Sibirien.

Kendall, Laurel, Barbara Mathé, and Thomas Ross Miller. 1997. *Drawing Shadows to Stone: The Photography of the Jesup North Pacific Expedition (1897– 1902)*. Seattle: University of Washington Press and American Museum of Natural History.

Leckert, Oriana. 2015. *Brooklyn Spaces: 50 Hubs of Culture and Creativity*. New York: The Monacelli Press.

Miller, Thomas Ross. 1992. "The Evidence of Instruments." *Anthropology & Humanism Quarterly* 17, no. 2: 49–60. https://doi.org/10.1525/ahu .1992.17.2.49.

Miller, Thomas Ross. 2011. "Ethnographic Termini: Of Moments and Metaphors." *Visual Anthropology Review (VAR)* 27, no. 1: 75–77. https://doi .org/10.1111/j.1548-7458.2011.01081.x.

Roberts, Mary Nooter, and Susan Vogel. 1994. *Exhibition-ism: Museums and African Art*. New York: The Museum for African Art.

Schildkrout, Enid, and Keim, Curtis A. 1990. *African Reflections: Art from Northeastern Zaire.* New York: American Museum of Natural History and University of Washington Press.

Ssorin-Chaikov, Nikolai, ed. 2013. "Ethnographic Conceptualism." In *Laboratorium: Russian Review of Social Research* #2. St. Petersburg: Centre for Independent Social Research.

Turk, Victoria. 2017. "This Is the Sound of Global Protest, from Trump to Brexit." *Wired,* August 7.

CHAPTER THIRTEEN

Engaging a Wider Audience with Fiction Film

Carylanna Taylor

I am an applied cultural anthropologist turned filmmaker. This chapter focuses on my experiences writing and producing *ANYA*, a contemporary sci-fi love story inspired by recent developments in anthropology and genetics. The story is about an infertile couple whose decision to have a child leads them to a research scientist, a genetically and culturally isolated community hiding in plain sight in New York City, and a life-changing question: Are they willing to have a gene-edited baby, no matter the cost?

I describe here how I came to apply cultural anthropology through film, how we gained unexpected support from genetics professionals, what I think is and isn't working in this film/anthropology intersection, and how I plan to apply lessons learned from *ANYA* to a new fiction project inspired by my own anthropological research.

DEVELOPING *ANYA*

My partner, Emmy-nominated filmmaker Jacob Akira Okada, and I began writing *ANYA* in May 2014. We had just finished our first project together, *Painting the Way to the Moon*, a feature documentary about a mathematician and artist whose work at NASA led to a new mode of space travel. We had enjoyed the challenge of communicating scientific concepts to a broader public and continued to be intrigued by how narratives of scientific discovery often gloss over the number of people and amount of chance involved in them. In *ANYA*, we set out to tell a story about scientific discovery from the perspective of the researchers and participants. Our broadest target audience was the same for both films: curious people eager to take a deeper dive into a topic based in anthropology, science, or current events that is rarely explored in film. As *ANYA* developed, our understanding of our audience evolved.

The initial drafts of *ANYA*'s screenplay grew from a set of questions that wouldn't have been out of place in one of my intro to anthropology classrooms. Could multiple species of humans be alive today? If so, how would we find them? If a genetically isolated group of humans some- how survived, how would they explain their inability to reproduce with members of the general population? What would their culture look like? To answer these questions in the script, we drew on my teaching and research experience and on our familiarity with New York City en- clave communities.

Even though it was easy to imagine *ANYA* sparking discussions in an- thropology classes, it was not our intention to create an educational tool. At most, I hoped that *ANYA* might challenge viewers' notions of cultural and genetic diversity or get them talking about gene editing ethics. As Jacob cautioned, it is extremely rare for a single film to change practices or beliefs. So, instead, we focused on telling a good story.

It's a little ironic that the first folks to embrace *ANYA* were educators. Though unintended, this is a direct consequence of treating research for *ANYA* as seriously as we would have for a documentary or anthro- pological research project. Our collaborations, conversations, and observations alongside genetics professionals (described below) led us to incorporate genetic testing, editing, and ethics into the script before they were part of larger public discussions. As a result, genetics profes- sionals and educators from high school to post grad see the film as a discussion starter for these hot-button topics.

We continue to get invitations to screen *ANYA* and participate in Q&As, panels, and podcasts, often alongside geneticists. For example, the University of Connecticut brought us in to screen and discuss the film with 300 students and faculty on their medical campus. Several

UConn faculty members incorporated *ANYA* into curriculum training for genetics counselors and other professionals. *ANYA* has also screened with Q&As at the Festival of Genomics in London and the Future of Health Summit in Slovakia. Films Media Group, a premiere educational distributor, picked up *ANYA* as one of their first fiction titles, making it available to stream in high school, college, and public libraries in the United States, Canada, and beyond. *ANYA* has also screened at small festivals in the United States and Europe.

It's harder to say at this time how well we're reaching a broader public of people interested in indie films and grounded sci-fi. Our reach has been limited by our lack of "names" (aka well-known cast or crew) and possibly by the subject matter. However, our reviews from the nonscientists who watch *ANYA* have been positive. On November 26, 2019, we made *ANYA* widely available on demand (Amazon, Apple, FandangoNow, Google Play, Vimeo, Vudu, Xbox) and DVD. During the release, we used reviews, articles, podcasts, and social media advertising to try to reach curious audiences of science and sci-fi enthusiasts. Throughout 2020, we used sales and marketing data to continue reaching out to broader audiences eager to discover thought-provoking entertainment.

ANTHROPOLOGIST TURNED FILMMAKER

I didn't set out to be a filmmaker. As a kid growing up in southwestern Pennsylvania, I was drawn to photography and storytelling and thought I might become a photojournalist. Instead, spending my junior year as a high school exchange student in Chile turned my focus to environmental issues in a global context. For 20 years, I studied sustainable rural development in the Americas through the lenses of Latin American studies and economics (BA, Penn State, 1997), development sociology (MS, Cornell, 2003), and applied cultural anthropology (PhD, University of South Florida [USF], 2011). Photography and stories were simply part of my toolkit for conducting and communicating research.

My first film was *Anthropology 2.0*, a short documentary for a USF visual anthropology class that two classmates, Suellen Regonini and Marc Hébert, and I filmed during the 2007 Society for Applied Anthropology meetings. We took turns setting up, conducting, and filming interviews. Marc showed me that most people don't mind being approached with a camera. Sue taught me nonlinear editing software. And our professor, Elizabeth Bird, introduced me to the ethics of filmmaking and the power of visual representation.

As much as I enjoyed the project, I didn't immediately become a filmmaker. I was too focused on my dissertation research on natural resource management within Honduran transnational families and on finding a job.

It wasn't until I met Jacob in 2012 that I began seeing film as a cool way to bring anthropology to a broader audience. I started out applying organizational and analytical skills learned from "producing" anthropological classes and studies to help Jacob and editor Adam Morrow produce *Painting the Way to the Moon*. In fall 2012, I gave feedback on drafts. In winter 2013, I helped write grants and run a successful crowd-sourcing campaign. In May 2013, after my visiting professorship ended, I moved to New York City to teach classes as an adjunct and field produce interviews and demonstrations for the documentary. Over the next year, I contributed to editing and took over distribution.

In May 2014, Jacob and I began writing *ANYA*, which more directly draws on anthropological understandings of culture, biology, diversity, and research. I started taking workshops and attending conferences to get a better grasp of fiction film writing and distribution. We wrote and produced three narrative shorts for practice. In summer 2016, we made the strategic decision that I would go full time with our small company, First Encounter Productions, in order to get *ANYA* off the ground. We filmed in summer 2017, finished the edit a year later, and released the film on demand and DVD in November 2019. I then chose to pursue an MFA in film producing at the American Film Institute Conservatory in Los Angeles, because being co-creator and business manager of *ANYA* has made me realize I have a lot to learn about the industry if I want to even more effectively apply anthropology through film.

RELATIONSHIPS ARE KEY

The primary relationship fueling my film work is my partnership with Jacob Akira Okada (NYU, BFA in film, 2002). Apart from a smattering of class and freelance projects, I designed and managed most of my classes, research, and writing alone. Finding a long-term writing and producing partner in Jacob has meant that, for the first time, I'm part of a creative and decision-making team. Our skill sets are complementary and allow us to row in the same direction even when working independently or experiencing creative differences. It's incredibly satisfying to co-create our projects and troubleshoot them together when problems arise. Even though I serve as the day-to-day manager of our company and films, having a sounding board and sharing the weight has allowed me to push harder and further than I could have on my own.

The list of relationships that made *ANYA* possible is long. For instance, because casting directors Anne Davison and John Ort believed in the script, they helped us find a talented cast even though we were unknown. The Librería Barco de Papel, a Spanish-language bookstore in Queens, allowed us to film inside and helped us recruit local extras. In all, 16 cast members, 34 extras, 47 production and postproduction crew members, 13 marketing and distribution companies or individuals, 14 musicians, a language advisor (fellow USF anthropology alum José Enrique Moreno Cortés), four science advisors, and another 143 individuals – supplying everything from a filming location to feedback – chose to be part of *ANYA*. Each time we've screened, be it at a festival, conference, or university, we've had one or more screening partners who took the time to review, host, and publicize *ANYA*. When they're able to pay for our travel or screening, our hosts also have to work with other gatekeepers at their institution to approve the screening and payment. And then there are all of the podcast hosts, reviewers, journalists, and viewers who've helped get out the word. Filmmaking truly is a team sport!

Our relationship with our science advisors has been particularly rewarding. In 2015, we reached out to the Science and Entertainment Exchange at the National Academy of Sciences for advice on the specific genetic mechanism leading to infertility in *ANYA*. They put us in touch with geneticists Ting Wu and Ruth McCole at Harvard Medical School (see Figure 13.1). They lent their research to the film, gave feedback on scripts, and introduced us to the Wu Lab and the Personal Genetics Education Project (pgEd), including Marnie Gilbert, ethicists Jeantine Lunshof, and CRISPR pioneer George Church. Ruth even wrote a short dialogue scene, choreographed the lab experiments shown in the film, and taught *ANYA* actors how to use real lab equipment. Ruth also introduced us to computational geneticist Andreas Pfenning, who later convinced Carnegie Mellon University to allow us

Figure 13.1. Taylor and science advisors meet at Harvard Medical School.

to film in his research lab under the supervision of grad student Alyssa Lawler. They and their colleagues' willingness to talk with us and include us in meetings, symposia, and congressional briefings allowed us to more accurately portray genetics and geneticists and to broach ethical discussions related to genetic testing and editing. Their collaboration is the main reason we had such strong early support from genetics professionals, science educators, and conferences such as the Festival of Genomics and Future of Health Summit.

Had I not studied applied anthropology at USF, I likely would not have seen applying anthropology through fiction film as a viable career path. Despite my early fears of somehow being "less than" because I chose not to pursue a more established path in academia or development consulting, many of my classmates and faculty have been very supportive. My former advisor, Rebecca Zarger, wrote my recommendation to a film conservatory. Kristina Baines and Victoria Costa have attended screenings, given feedback, and included me in this volume. Medical anthropologist Jennifer Syvertsen shows her classes *ANYA* and *Curtis* (Jacob's award-winning documentary short on hospice care that premiered in 2004 at Sundance). During a Skype Q&A with her class, I felt like we were continuing a discussion from our legal and ethical seminar a decade earlier. Jason Miller has included me in panels at the American Anthropological Association (AAA) and the Society for Applied Anthropology (SfAA). At these meetings, I've met new colleagues who have introduced me to new ways to reach a broader public through film, such as ethnographic fiction. I'm grateful to the AAA and SfAA for hosting test screenings of *ANYA* and a filmmaking-for-anthropologists workshop, as well as to the National Association of Practicing Anthropologists (NAPA) for publishing my *Anthropology News* article on *ANYA* and inviting me to participate in their career expo. This support from the anthropological community makes me feel that there is value in applying anthropology through fiction film.

GETTING IT DONE

My primary modality is feature-length films viewed online, on DVD, in a theater, or in a classroom. Creating those films requires a variety of technologies, including filmmaking equipment and software.

We wrote *ANYA* using 3 x 5 cards, a whiteboard, and occasionally Google Sheets or Docs to brainstorm and outline the script. We wrote in tandem in WriterDuet, free online software that helps structure and format the script.

For project management, I used Google Drive, Docs, Sheets, and Calendar as well as Adobe Acrobat, Microsoft Office, email, a paper calendar, and to-do lists on whiteboards. During preproduction, we used specialized budgeting and scheduling software. During production, we briefly used a team workspace (Basecamp) but ended up defaulting to email and text because it was easier to use on the fly.

Each film requires a different set of equipment. In *ANYA*, we chose a documentary style approach of using a small DSLR-sized camera, a one-person sound crew, and existing lighting sometimes supplemented with light panels. This small footprint allowed us to largely disappear in public spaces and adjust quickly on set. We created the look of the film through location, wardrobe, and production design choices. Future projects may require larger footprints with more complex setups.

In post-production, Jacob and I edited the film in Adobe Premiere and used After Effects and Endcrawl to create the credits. Our team used specialized software for color correction (DaVinci Resolve) and

Figure 13.2. Filmmakers Taylor and Okada with actors at Coney Island.

sound sweetening (Avid) as well as Google Sheets to track music choices and licensing.

Though feature films are our primary modality, in the process of marketing and distributing *ANYA*, we created a plethora of secondary modalities. We hired Wheelhouse Creative to create the trailer and Indika to create the poster and "key art" (covers and thumbnails used on social media and distribution platforms). From these, we used Premiere, Photoshop, and Illustrator to create additional clips and art for social media and ads. Photographs from screenings and productions also found their way to our website and social media. I also created an "electronic press kit" – basically a combination of project summaries, bios, stills, and behind-the-scenes images and clips that press can use to write articles.

Our distributor drew from these materials to place *ANYA* on streaming platforms and create the DVD cover. We generated captions and subtitles for the trailer and film using a combination of YouTube Studio and specialized companies. Our publicists and I used the trailer, poster, and press kit to create a distribution press release and contacted journalists and potential reviewers by phone, email, and social media.

These folks then created reviews, articles, and podcasts related to the film. Jacob and I were interviewed for many of these. To help get out the word, I also wrote several newsletter and blog posts, filmed a Skype interview with our science advisor, Ruth McCole, and participated in panels and Q&As. Our social media specialist used all of these resources along with screening photos to create posts on Instagram and Facebook. I used them to create posts on Twitter, present at conferences, give public talks to science enthusiasts, populate First Encounter Productions' YouTube channel, and maintain *ANYA*'s website (anyamovie.com). At this point, the writing about *ANYA* exceeds the length of the script!

TOUGH DECISIONS, TOUGH MOMENTS

In January 2017, Jacob and I faced a decision: we could either spend a year looking for money from investors or produce *ANYA* with earnings from our freelance work. We'd been writing and rewriting for two and a half years, and while we believed we had a unique project that was generating interest, it was not quite checking all the right boxes for gatekeepers at screenplay and grant competitions, perhaps because of the science focus or genre. (We would later have a similar experience with major film festivals, where we seemed to be a perennial "runner up.") Even though Jacob has a long list of documentary credits for directing, editing, and cinematography, we were both outsiders to the narrative world and simply didn't have the social networks to recruit the well-known executive producer or actor that we seemed to need to get to the next level of funding or recognition.

I was considering going back to adjunct teaching or freelance research. I couldn't justify another year full time in film without pay. Neither of us wanted to continue as things were or to abandon the project. When we realized we'd both be free from March through August of 2017, we decided to produce *ANYA* on our own. Our first step was to rewrite the script to drop the production budget from $2 million to $140,000. A film production company based in LA invested $20,000, which helped us secure our casting directors, cast, and fiscal sponsor. Our savings and a business loan covered the gap. We knew this wasn't the ideal way to finance a film, but we also knew that successfully completing a narrative feature would open doors for the next project. We were investing in our own careers and in the future of First Encounter Productions. Moreover, rentals, sales, and hosted screenings would help us recoup our investment. Positive professional and audience reviews would also build our filmmaking CV and make it easier to find funding and talent for the next project. The relationships previously described also provided a range of nonmonetary support.

The experience of collaborating with and being embraced by genetics professionals and science communicators has been personally rewarding. Those relationships, along with the scientific accuracy seen in *ANYA*, are testimony to the skills of trust building, interviewing, and observation that I developed as an anthropologist.

> *The experience of collaborating with and being embraced by genetics professionals and science communicators has been personally rewarding. Those relationships, along with the scientific accuracy seen in ANYA, are testimony to the skills of trust building, interviewing, and observation that I developed as an anthropologist.*

Many of the challenges I encountered with *ANYA* were typical for an indie film, such as wearing multiple hats, becoming a small business owner, navigating unions, taxes, laws, incentives, and insurance, as well as finding money, cast, crew, and locations. While titles like *The Filmmaker's Handbook* give indie filmmakers a great overview of what to expect, partnering with an experienced producer increases the chance of success.

Other challenges were more particular to being an anthropologist making her first fiction film. Being a newcomer to narrative film, I had a lot to learn about "set culture." This made hiring and managing the crew more difficult. Narrative sets tend to have large crews with clearly delineated, hierarchical jobs so that everyone knows their assigned roles based on job titles. We went into production with too poor an understanding of this hierarchy and too large and inexperienced a crew. Three days into a 16-day shoot, we were falling behind and about to lose the production. We revamped with a smaller footprint. Jacob took over shooting as well as directing. I went from "writer on set" to "producer on set" while I was still learning the difference between a first assistant director, second assistant director, and production coordinator. Fortunately, our unit production manager, Ashley Nicole Rosenberg, and the new crew helped me through it.

In my experience, filming is like fieldwork: prepare as best you can and learn fast once you hit the ground to make it easier to deal with the inevitable unexpected things.

One of my biggest challenges on *ANYA* was learning to summarize the project in the right language and tone. I first discovered the issue during an elevator pitch exercise at Stowe Story Labs. My focus was too heavy on science, anthropology, and concepts and too light on emotional journey. I was privileging head over heart – as is typical in academic papers and classes. Although I got better, this problem continued in writing "log lines" (40- to 70-word summaries of the film) and "synopses" (one- to five-paragraph story summaries).

> *Filming is like fieldwork: prepare as best you can and learn fast once you hit the ground to make it easier to deal with the inevitable unexpected things.*

To some reviewers' tastes, this tension is also visible in the film. I think they're reacting to our decision to show both the couple's and the geneticist's journey. It may be that emphasizing one or the other might have worked better in this modality (an 80-minute feature film). We and our main characters were driven by curiosity. Unfortunately, viewers are more likely to connect with emotion than intellect. While *ANYA* has both, an argument can be made that we might have had an easier time with festivals and general audiences had we put greater emphasis on emotion in our promotional materials and the film itself. I take heart that the mix seems to be right for the genetics professionals, anthropologists, and science educators who see *ANYA* as a discussion starter. A film can't be all things to all people – but I want to be more effective next time at shedding my "Vulcan" exterior and carrying viewers along for an emotional as well as intellectual journey.

FINAL THOUGHTS

ANYA is a cool, timely, thought-provoking story told with good acting and production values and relatively little money. It's found a core audience and will no doubt find others. It's starting discussions. On these counts, *ANYA* has met or exceeded our vision.

There are things we could have done better. We had to make some changes in production and editing that reshaped the story in ways that

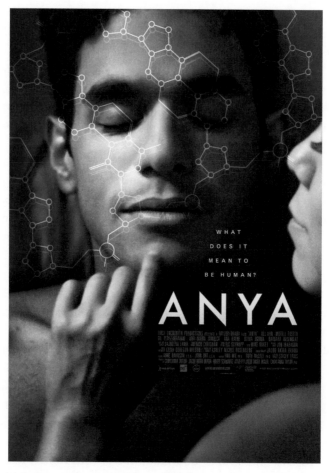

Figure 13.3. Promotional poster for ANYA.

seem to work better for science-minded folks than a general audience. A few reviewers found the film more convoluted than I had hoped. It's hard to know if viewers are tripped up by the science (which we worked hard to make accessible), the documentary style filming, the intentionally unanswered questions, or the complexity of the story. It's hard to know if ironing out some of the bumps would improve our reach to general audiences without sacrificing the story. I do know that we're never going to please everyone.

Overall, I am pleased with the film and our reach thus far. I am a bit concerned that we may have made a film so "us" that we're mostly preaching to the choir. Considering our investment and experience, I think this is okay, if not great. However, if I want my next project to be bigger in budget or impact, I have to learn to reach further.

BEYOND *ANYA*

As of spring 2022, I'm in my last semester as a producing fellow in the American Film Institute Conservatory. I chose to pursue an MFA so that my future projects would be more effective and have a broader reach than *ANYA*. Among the projects I'm developing, the closest to my heart is a television series loosely inspired by my 2000–2015 anthropological research with Honduran transnational families. The project, currently titled *Involuntary Departures*, focuses on a young woman who must decide whether to avenge her grandfather's murder or run for her life to the relative safety of the United States. By dramatizing and fictionalizing accounts captured during fieldwork, I hope to illustrate some of the structural forces that undermine rural livelihoods and drive migration.

My goal is to tell a story that is true enough to life to resonate with Central American farmers and migrants while being broadly appealing enough to pull in viewers who wouldn't typically watch an immigration documentary. I'm finding that the challenge is to let theory and analysis take a back seat to the emotional journey of a compelling character. For audiences to get a glimpse of my critique of the modern world system as it applies to migration, they'll first need to be taken on a thrilling and emotional journey led by a compelling protagonist. In getting across anthropological concepts through fiction films, I'm learning that the story must always come first.

Another lesson from *ANYA* and my prior film work is that well-established or high-profile collaborators help projects get funded, accepted into festivals, and seen by audiences online or in the theater. For instance, Neil deGrasse Tyson (*Cosmos*) appears in Jacob's and my documentary *Painting the Way to the Moon*. His presence at a screening made the difference between getting free publicity in the form of a local news article and having to pay for ads. Similarly, a beloved actor or executive producer can make the difference toward getting into a major festival or not. In doc and fiction, star power helps.

I'm still learning what kinds of movies resonate and how to focus on an emotional journey while telling a story grounded in anthropology. One thing I have learned is that in writing fiction – be it a movie or a novel – the primary goal must be to tell a good story – to entertain. From there, the value of the fictional work is largely in the eye of the beholder.

I might think about what I'd like viewers to experience or learn and try to craft and distribute the story in a way that puts it in front of those people, but it's ultimately out of my control who will discover or find value in the art I create. If I try to "educate" (or appear to be trying to educate), I risk alienating those who are just looking for a film or television series to entertain them, thereby limiting my potential audience.

It's ultimately out of my control who will discover or find value in the art I create. If I try to "educate" (or appear to be trying to educate), I risk alienating those who are just looking for a film or television series to entertain them, limiting my potential audience.

Part of the issue is that, unlike a class session or paper, a feature film can only communicate one, or possibly two, big ideas. More than that and the film feels confusing or didactic. Ninety minutes might seem like a long time, but fiction film is a far more indirect mode of communicating than documentary filmmaking or anthropological writing. The values or insights shared need to seep in through the story, through the entertainment. Recognizing and learning to work within these limitations has been one of the biggest challenges of transitioning from academia to film.

In the case of *Involuntary Departures*, for example, I want to craft a story that will capture the imagination of US and Latin American teens and adults who are curious about the experience of living in rural Central America or curious why a young person might abandon a home they love for the risky journey to the United States. To have a chance at positively contributing to conversations around migration, race, and sustainability, the project will need to be entertaining and engaging enough to reach far beyond those already interested in migration. To do more than "preach to the choir" and to reach a broader public, I will need a good team and established distribution partners.

In sum, applying anthropology through fiction film has a lot of potential, but it is also a time- and resource-intensive medium shaped by many considerations beyond the ideas or messages a filmmaker wishes to share. Movies and television are both art and business. A producer might call them a "high risk, high reward" approach to engaging a wider audience.

FOR DISCUSSION

1 What kinds of anthropological concepts or lessons learned can be best communicated through fictional storytelling?
2 Audience reactions to fiction films might be similar to as well as different from audience reactions to anthropological writing and documentary film. What are useful things to consider when deciding which mode to pursue?
3 There are risks and rewards in pursuing a larger audience by fictionalizing data, stories, and understandings gathered through anthropological research. How can a fictionalized project "do justice" to anthropological research?
4 Feature film is described as emotionally driven while anthropological research is said to be theoretically driven. Of the anthropological questions that most interest you, which might make for the most compelling fictional film or TV series? How might you go about getting it made?

REFERENCE

Ascher, S., and E. Pincus. 2007. *The Filmmaker's Handbook: A Comprehensive Guide for the Digital Age.* New York: Penguin.

CHAPTER FOURTEEN

LET US DO MORE THAN HOPE:

comics, complexity, & an anthropology in pictures and words

Sally Campbell Galman

Using comics in anthropology is about making things MORE COMPLEX, not more simple!

Anthropology knows that "simple" is a lie, and while comics can provide increased accessibility–this is not about a faster consumption.

Graphic anthropology is meant to simultaneously COMPLICATE & CLARIFY without simplifying, ELEGANTLY sticking in your craw.

For some context, I'm the artist behind the Shane the Lone Ethnographer comics and loads of other stuff.

I CAN DO THIS!

I'm an academic and an artist, and this comic will tell the story of how those identities fit together, how I use comics in my scholarly work, and how I believe the arts and arts-based research can make LIGHT in the darkness. Buckle up.

What I do has a couple different names:

♥ See Galman 2021a, 2021b; kuttner, Sousanis, & Weaver-Hightower, 2018. ♥

HELLO
my name is

Arts-Based
Research

HELLO
my name is

Comics-Based
Research

↑ ABR uses the tools of art-making (visual, performance, creative writing, etc.) to collect and/or analyze data, and/or share research with the public.

↑ CBR is a special type of ABR that employs the tools of comic art for data gathering & analysis, and also presenting research to the public.

I have choreographed a dance to tell about my research!

I drew a comic to communicate my research findings!

Using the arts to share research "give[s] empathy and insight into experience" (Weaver-Hightower, 2017). They convey emotion accessibly, but with complexity.

1. How did you get started?

I was always an artist, and as a student at Grinnell College I had a weekly strip that won a big fancy prize and was made into a book.

But when I started my PhD program, I thought I had to Put Away All Childish Things, like

DRAWING STUFF   FEELINGS

BEING A WOMAN

So I could fit into the shape of a

SERIOUS ACADEMIC.

But then my advisor, Marki, suggested that art should not be a separate, *nights-* and *-weekends* SIDE HUSTLE but rather the center of an integrated life.

A bifurcated life just isn't healthy!

Even if it looks really different from what you see in most of academia.

It took YEARS of writing and drawing and *Suspended Disbelief* to get to a place where I believed in myself and that my work was legitimate.

OVER TENURE & PROMOTION

WHIRLING VORTICES OF WORRY

WAVE UPON WAVE OF DOUBT.

HAND-LETTERING HUNDREDS OF PAGES

ee cummings wrote: "to be nobody-but-yourself in a world that is doing its best, night and day, to make you everybody else means fighting the hardest battle which any human being can fight and never stop fighting."

"Be true to your own secret Knowledge" -SEAMUS HEANEY

A lot of this shape-shifting is made possible by INTERDISCIPLINARITY Because drawing from not just my own home discipline of Anthropology but also lots of other places encourages ECLECTICISM

2. But HOW do you do this work? What techniques and modalities do you use?

That's a question I get frequently, and I try to answer it clearly to do what I can to DEMYSTIFY the arts-based research process.

hey

ECLECTICISM WORKS! consider the caterpillar synchlora aerata decorates its body with bits of flowers that both camouflage and nourish.

Ich hath loste myn SANITYE.

I used to say my technique was not too dissimilar from that of a medieval monk illuminating manuscripts by dim candlelight for hours and hours and hours by hand, praying the whole time that I don't spill the ink or make a mistake or have to start all over again and LOSE MY MIND.

But then I got a Tablet ♡ and things got a lot easier. I still sketch rough drafts out by hand and scan them in to refine digitally on the tablet. It was a steep learning curve but worth it.

NO MORE SOAKING MY HANDS IN PANS OF ICE!

2. BIG ROUGH DRAFT

plus

1. Rough ideas in little notebook

all my analytic & fieldnotes

into

BIG FANCY SCANNER

3. SCANNING & UPLOADING

4. Editing & refining on the tablet.

& saved to the cloud.

3. But how do you make all this hybridity and eclecticism WORK on a practical level?

SAVE LIVES: Having other people's work to point to and build upon is both legitimizing and a source of support and connection. And senior folks should try their best to **MAKE ART** break trail or simply hold up junior scholars' work in this arena. **FIND WAYS TO MAKE SPACE!** → As journal editors, we made a "creative section" in AEQ.

"if my art has nothing to do with people's pain and sorrow, what is 'art' for?" - Ai Wei Wei

HOPE
COMFORT
INSPIRATION
STRENGTH
LOVE

Ann Lamott (1995) said this about reading and writing, and I think it also holds true for scholarship: Our work can "decrease our sense of isolation. They deepen and widen and expand our sense of life: they feed the soul...

It's like singing on a boat during a terrible storm at sea. You cant stop the raging storm, but singing can change the hearts and spirits of the people who are together on that ship" (p. 237)

Anthropology asks what it means to be a human being and arts-based ethnography asks how we can all become more fully human, and to affirm others' humanity

This is where those two hands come in: one brings hope and the other exhorts us to do MORE THAN HOPE.
(Eisner, 2008)

Eisner (2008) writes that we must, as arts-based scholars,

"do more than hope. Let us embark on those studies of human action that reveal aspects of human experience and behavior that intuitively are difficult to deny." (p.11)

And we must realize the promise of arts-based work by drawing on its unique strengths:

As Barone & Eisner (2012) write, this is "method designed to enlarge human understanding... to enable an individual to secure an empathetic participation in the lives of others" (p8-9)

WHILE SIMULTANEOUSLY AFFIRMING THAT "ART IS NOT A MIRROR TO REFLECT REALITY BUT A HAMMER WITH WHICH TO SHAPE IT."
(BRECHT)

"TYRANTS ALWAYS FEAR ART."

—Iris Murdoch

AND IT IS THAT SUBVERSIVE HYBRIDITY & COMPLEXITY, THAT UNRULY BOUNDARY-CROSSING, THAT I LOVE.

(Baba Yaga is my favorite man-eating, forest-dwelling badass of folklore, and also my favorite symbol of the gendered, creative margins. Her hybridity makes her an "outlier with power" (Clifford, 2017).)

I do also write lots of *funny* things — but this [like this!] →

SHANE THE LONE ETHNOGRAPHER

Second Edition

SALLY CAMPBELL GALMAN

too-humor, can be unruly and prickly, and is part of that same two-handed vision → making learning about ethnography more fun and accessible. Art heals this way, too, and laughter can be liberation.*

Wow. I had no idea. I've never read anything like these stories.

comic ethnography

As Leavy (2019) writes, "aesthetics are linked to advancing care and compassion" and self-other knowledge (p. 5).

The unique accessibility of comics—one that *clarifies* but does not *simplify*— is part of this vision: Much of my work tells the stories of marginalized children in challenging political environments. These stories can be hard to hear and harder to tell ...

and for this reason I want readers to read *and* FEEL ...

*Edward Abbey said, "A distrust of wit is the beginning of tyranny."

6. What are the challenges in doing this work?

But it is worth it.

7. At the end of the day, what are the LESSONS LEARNED?

The lessons I've learned as a working artist and academic are too numerous to list here but I will give you the TOP THREE

1. DON'T LET WORRIES ABOUT BEING DIFFERENT GRIND YOU DOWN. SOMEONE OUT THERE NEEDS YOUR WORK.

Believe in your work and the value of creativity, even when it seems risky.

Where do you think I came from?

2. READING HELPS! Read WIDELY. About EVERYTHING. That's where the powerful metaphors and images come from!

3. GIVE YOURSELF SOME CREDIT. As e.e. cummings said, any idiot out there can destroy—destruction is easy. But to make something, to create, is to heal the world, to do more than hope, to *also* take the emotional and intellectual risks to try

Sally Campbell Galman is an anthropologist and visual artist and Professor of Child and Family Studies at the University of Massachusetts-Amherst. www.sallycampbellgalman.com

To Recap:

- Don't be afraid to do things differently in your work and writing.
- Following what sustains you and your work can be challenging but worth it!
- The arts and arts-based research can be healing and also powerful.
- The arts can combine with ethnography in lots of fruitful ways.

⑦ Ask yourself: How might venturing/reading/creating into eclectic areas enrich your work as an anthropologist?

⑦ What creative experiments might you try?

HOPE
COMFORT
INSPIRATION
STRENGTH
LOVE

REFERENCES

Abbey, E. 1989. *A Voice Crying in the Wilderness (Vox Clamantis in Deserto): Notes from a Secret Journal.* London: St. Martin's.

Abramovic, M. 2016. *Walk through Walls: A Memoir.* New York: Crown.

Barone, T., and E.W. Eisner. 2012. *Arts-Based Research.* London: SAGE.

Cavna, M. 2019. "The New York Times Cuts All Political Cartoons, and Cartoonists Are Not Happy." *Washington Post,* June 11. https://www .washingtonpost.com/arts-entertainment/2019/06/11/new-york-times-cuts -all-political-cartoons-cartoonists-are-not-happy/?utm_term=.9488910fd37c.

Clifford, M. 2017. "The Enduring Allure of Baba Yaga, an Ancient Swamp Witch Who Loves to Eat People." *Vice,* November 2. https://www.vice.com /en_us/article/evbbjj/the-enduring-allure-of-baba-yaga-an-ancient-swamp -witch-who-loves-to-eat-people.

cummings, e.e. 1958. "A Poet's Advice to Students." In *e.e. cummings: A Miscellany,* ed. G.J. Firmage, 363–65. New York: Liveright.

EASA (European Association of Social Anthropologists). 2015. "Why Anthropology Matters." https://www.easaonline.org/publications/policy /why_en.shtml.

Eisner, E.W. 2008. "Art and Knowledge." In *Handbook of the Arts in Qualitative Research: Perspectives, Methodologies, Examples, and Issues,* ed. J.G. Knowles and A.R. Cole, 3–12. London: SAGE.

Galman, S.C. 2018. *Shane, the Lone Ethnographer: A Beginner's Guide to Ethnographic Research,* 2nd ed. Lanham: Rowman & Littlefield.

Galman, S.C. 2021a. "Follow the Headlights: On Comics-Based Data Analysis." In *Analyzing and Interpreting Qualitative Data: After the Interview,* ed. C. Vanover, P. Mihas, and J. Saldaña. London: SAGE.

Galman, S.C. 2021b. "Ghostly Presences Out There: Transgender Girls and Their Families in the Time of COVID." *Girlhood Studies* 13, no. 3: 79–97. https://doi.org/10.3167/ghs.2020.130307.

Gerber, N., E. Templeton, G. Chilton, M.C. Liebman, E. Manders, and M. Shim. 2012. "Arts-Based Research as a Pedagogical Approach to Studying Intersubjectivity in the Creative Art Therapies." *Journal of Applied Arts & Health* 3, no. 1: 29–48. https://doi.org/10.1386/jaah.3.1.39_1.

Hart, B. 2015. "4 Cartoonists Killed in Attack on Charlie Hebdo Newspaper." *Huffington Post,* January 7. https://www.huffpost.com/entry/cartoonists -killed-attack_n_6428962.

Heaney, S. 2005. [Untitled]. In *Take This Advice,* ed. S. Bark, 80–87. New York: Simon & Schuster.

Kuttner, P., N. Sousanis, and M.B. Weaver-Hightower. 2018. "How to Draw Comics the Scholarly Way: Creating Comics-Based Research in the Academy." In *Handbook of Arts-Based Research,* ed. P. Leavy, 396–423. New York: Guilford Press.

Lamott, A. 1995. *Bird by Bird.* New York: Penguin.

Leavy, P. 2019. "Introduction to Arts-Based Research." In *Handbook of Arts-Based Research*, ed. P. Leavy, 3–21.New York: Guilford Press.

Murdoch, I. 2016. *Living on Paper: Letters from Iris Murdoch 1934–1995*. Ed. A. Horner and A. Rowe. Princeton: Princeton University Press.

Siers, K. 2019. "This Time, the 'Failing New York Times' Really Is Failing, Big Time." American Association of Editorial Cartoonists, June 11.

Weaver-Hightower, M.B. 2017. "Losing Thomas & Ella: A Father's Story (A Research Comic)." *Journal of Medical Humanities* 38, no. 3: 215–30. https://doi.org/10.1007/s10912-015-9359-z.

Weiwei, A., A. Cohen, and A. Klayman. 2012. *Ai Weiwei: Never Sorry*. Expressions United Media.

Contributors

Leslie Aiello's interests are the evolution of human adaptation and the broader issues of evolutionary theory, life history, energetics, and the evolution of the brain and cognition. She is president emerita, Wenner-Gren Foundation for Anthropological Research, and professor emerita, University College London.

Kristina Baines is an associate professor of anthropology at City University of New York (CUNY) Guttman Community College, affiliated faculty at CUNY Graduate School of Public Health and Health Policy, and the founder and director of anthropology at Cool Anthropology.

Elizabeth Challinor is currently researching refugee reception in Portugal (New University of Lisbon, FCT project PTDC/FER-ETC/30378/2017). She has published on the anthropology of development in Cape Verde and on migrant mothering in Portugal, where her emerging work focuses on migrant and refugee engagement with the law.

Chip Colwell is the founding editor-in-chief of *SAPIENS*, a digital magazine about anthropology for the general public.

Victoria Costa is a creative technologist and community organizer, and the founder and director of cool at Cool Anthropology.

Gregg Deal (Pyramid Lake Paiute Tribe) is a provocative contemporary artist who challenges Western perceptions of Indigenous people, touching on issues of race, history, and stereotypes. Through his work, Deal critically examines issues and tells stories of decolonization and appropriation that affect Indian country.

Celia Emmelhainz is the anthropology and qualitative librarian at UC Berkeley. She has an MA in anthropology from Texas A&M and an MLIS in information science from Kent State. Her research focuses on anthropological archiving, qualitative data, and working conditions in libraries in the United States and Central Asia.

Agustín Fuentes is a professor of anthropology at Princeton University researching human evolution, multispecies anthropology, and structures of race and racism. Fuentes' books include *Race, Monogamy, and Other Lies They Told You: Busting Myths about Human Nature* and *Why We Believe: Evolution and the Human Way of Being.*

Sally Campbell Galman is an anthropologist and visual and performance artist whose research focuses on comics-based, arts-based study of young children and gender diversity. She is a professor of child and family studies at the University of Massachusetts.

Vanesa Giraldo Gartner is a medical anthropologist with primary area specialization in Colombia and a research focus on the armed conflict, peace transitions, and intercultural health. She is a PhD candidate at the University of Massachusetts' Department of Anthropology and a researcher at the Colombian and German Institute for Peace.

Krista M. Harper is a professor in the Department of Anthropology and the School of Public Policy at the University of Massachusetts Amherst. She uses ethnographic and participatory action research methods to study urban environments, food justice, and social infrastructure in Hungary, Portugal, and the United States.

Castriela Hernández-Reyes is a Black/decolonial feminist scholar, activist, and president of Colombia's Afro-researchers Association – ACIAFRO. A PhD candidate in anthropology at UMass Amherst, she studies how race, gender embodiment, and class intersect in wartime and are tied to colonial logics of racism.

Caitlin Homrich-Knieling is the deep canvass coordinator with We the People Michigan, based in Detroit. She received degrees from UMass Amherst (MA, Anthropology, 2016) and Central Michigan University (BA, 2014). She is originally from the "Thumb" of Michigan and does community organizing for multiracial liberation.

Sarah C. Hutton is the interim dean of Libraries at the University of Massachusetts Amherst. She administers the W.E.B. Du Bois and Science and Engineering Library on the Amherst campus, and the Wadsworth Library on the Mt. Ida campus in Newton, MA.

Kristin Koptiuch is a cool urban ethnographer who tries to practice anthro as much performance art as social science. She is an emerita associate professor at Arizona State University–West, where she spent more than two decades exploring the un-urban urbanism of Phoenix and engaging students in learning-from-the-city courses.

Daniel H. Lende is an associate professor of anthropology at the University of South Florida. He co-founded Neuroanthropology.net and has worked on online engagement and public impact using blogs, wikis, and Instagram. His research spans medical, psychological, and biocultural anthropology.

Kerry Hawk Lessard is an applied medical anthropologist working in the field of urban Indian health. Her work focuses on historical trauma and creating culturally grounded health programs that promote healing. She is the descendant of Irish, Assiniboine, and Shawnee peoples.

Gwendolen Lynch, formerly Gawain, has spent a lifetime architecting and creating things, from global communities to technological solutions at scale. She has a keen interest in cross-disciplinary collaboration and science communication. Caring for a scurry of squirrels nesting around her home keeps her world in perspective.

John McCreery is a *PopAnth* writing coach. Partner and Vice-President, The Word Works, Ltd. Born 1944. BA Philosophy, Michigan State

University, 1966. PhD Anthropology, Cornell University, 1973. Anthropologist, adman, activist, independent scholar. Studied magicians in Taiwan. Joined the guild in Japan.

Laura Miller is the Ei'ichi Shibusawa-Seigo Arai Endowed Professor of Japanese Studies and professor of history at the University of Missouri–St. Louis. She is currently doing research on the occult and divination industry in Japan.

Tom Miller is an anthropologist, curator, radio artist, and composer. His research encompasses sound, music, shamanism, Indigenous histories, museums, archives, media, and public art.

James Mullooly is a professor of anthropology and director of the Institute of Public Anthropology at California State University Fresno. Author of *Anthropology Applied to Everyday Life*, James' research foci include entrepreneurship, education, and workforce development. He has worked in Jamaica, Mali, Egypt, and the United States.

Elena Sesma is an assistant professor in the Department of Anthropology at the University of Kentucky. She received her PhD in anthropology at the University of Massachusetts, Amherst, specializing in historical archaeology, and her BA in anthropology and women's studies from the University of Maryland, College Park

Carylanna Taylor is an applied cultural anthropologist (PhD, University of South Florida, 2011) and filmmaker (MFA, Producing, American Film Institute Conservatory, 2022). Her films, including the feature *ANYA* (2019), draw on twenty years of teaching and researching migration and environment in the United States and Latin America.

Erin B. Taylor is an anthropologist of finance with a PhD from the University of Sydney. She is the founder of Finthropology, a research consultancy specializing in insights into people's financial behavior. Erin is the author of the monograph *Materializing Poverty: How the Poor Transform Their Lives*.

Maria D. Vesperi is a professor of anthropology at New College of Florida and executive coordinating editor of *Anthropology Now*. A former trustee of the Poynter Institute and *Tampa Bay Times* staffer, her publications include *City of Green Benches* and the co-edited volumes *Anthropology off the Shelf* and *The Culture of Long-Term Care.*

R. Scott Wilson is a cultural anthropologist who teaches courses on visual anthropology, new media, and identity theory at CSU-Long Beach. His current project explores the relationship between space, emotion, and the techniques of immersion in virtual reality experiences and non-linear documentaries.

Index